The Life-Giving Power of the Cross

Sharing in Christ's Victory

Jeanne Kun

The Word Among Us Press
7115 Guilford Drive
Frederick, MD 21704
www.wau.org

15 14 13 12 11 1 2 3 4 5

ISBN 978-1-59325-180-2

Nihil Obstat: The Rev. Michael Morgan, Chancellor
Censor Librorum
November 2, 2010

Imprimatur: +Most Rev. Victor Galeone
Bishop of St. Augustine
November 2, 2010

Scripture passages contained herein are from the New Revised Standard Version Bible: Catholic Edition, copyright © 1989, 1993, Division of Christian Education of the National Council of the Churches of Christ in the United States of America. Used by permission. All rights reserved.

The English translation of Non-Biblical Readings from The Liturgy of the Hours, copyright © 1974, International Committee on English in the Liturgy, Inc. All rights reserved.

Excerpts from the English translation of the *Catechism of the Catholic Church* for use in the United States of America, copyright © 1994, United States Catholic Conference, Inc. – Libreria Editrice Vaticana. Used with permission.

Cover Design: Heather Raffa
Text Design: David Crosson

Made and printed in the United States of America.

Library of Congress Cataloging-in-Publication Data

Kun, Jeanne, 1951-
   The life-giving power of the cross : sharing in Christ's victory / Jeanne Kun.
      p. cm.
   ISBN 978-1-59325-180-2
   1. Jesus Christ--Crucifixion--Textbooks. 2. Jesus Christ--Resurrection--Textbooks. I. Title.
   BT453.K86 2011
   232.96'3--dc22
                                        2010037937

Contents

Welcome to
The Word Among Us
Keys to the Bible

Have you ever lost your keys? Everyone seems to have at least one "lost keys" story to tell. Maybe you had to break a window of your house or wait for the auto club to let you into your car. Whatever you had to do probably cost you—in time, energy, money, or all three. Keys are definitely important items to have on hand!

The guides in The Word Among Us Keys to the Bible series are meant to provide you with a handy set of keys that can "unlock" the treasures of the Scriptures for you. Scripture is God's living word. Within its pages we meet the Lord. So as we study and meditate on Scripture and unlock its many treasures, we discover the riches it contains—and in the process, we grow in intimacy with God.

Since 1982, *The Word Among Us* magazine has helped Catholics develop a deeper relationship with the Lord through daily meditations that bring the Scriptures to life. More than ever, Catholics today desire to read and pray with the Scriptures, and many have begun to form small faith-sharing groups to explore the Bible together.

We designed the Keys to the Bible series after conducting a survey among our magazine readers to learn what they wanted in a Catholic Bible study. We found that they were looking for easy-to-understand, faith-filled materials that approach Scripture from a clearly Catholic perspective. Moreover, they wanted a Bible study that shows them how they can apply what they learn from Scripture to their everyday lives. They also asked for sessions that they can complete in an hour or two.

Our goal was to design a simple, easy-to-use Bible study guide that is also challenging and thought provoking. We hope that this guide fulfills those admittedly ambitious goals. We are confident, however, that taking the time to go through this guide—whether by yourself, with a friend, or in a small group—will be a worthwhile endeavor that will bear fruit in your life.

How to Use the Guides in This Series

The study guides in the Keys to the Bible series are divided into six sessions that each deal with a particular aspect of the topic. Before starting the first session, take the time to read the introduction, which sets the stage for the sessions that follow.

Whether you use this guide for personal reflection and study, as part of a faith-sharing group, or as an aid in your prayer time, be sure to begin each session with prayer. Ask God to open his word to you and to speak to you personally. Read each Scripture passage slowly and carefully. Then, take as much time as you need to meditate on the passage and pursue any thoughts it brings to mind. When you are ready, move on to the accompanying commentary, which offers various insights into the text.

Two sets of questions are included in each session to help you "mine" the Scripture passage and discover its relevance to your life. Those under the heading "Understand!" focus on the text itself and help you grasp what it means. Occasionally a question allows for a variety of answers and is meant to help you explore the passage from several angles. "Grow!" questions are intended to elicit a personal response by helping you examine your life in light of the values and truths that you uncover through your study of the Scripture passage and its setting. Under the headings "Reflect!" and "Act!" we offer suggestions to help you respond concretely to the challenges posed by the passage.

Finally, pertinent quotations from the Fathers of the Church as well as insights from contemporary writers appear throughout each session. Coupled with relevant selections from the *Catechism of the Catholic Church* and information about the history, geography, and culture of first-century Palestine, these selections (called "In the Spotlight") add new layers of understanding and insight to your study.

As is true with any learning resource, this study will benefit you the most when you write your answers to the questions in the spaces provided. The simple act of writing can help you formulate your thoughts more clearly—and will also give you a record of your reflections and spiritual growth that you can return to in the future to see how much God has accomplished in your life. End your reading or study with a prayer thanking God for what you have learned—and ask the Holy Spirit to guide you in living out the call you have been given as a Christian in the world today.

Although the Scripture passages to be studied and the related verses for your reflection are printed in full in each guide (from the New Revised Standard Version: Catholic Edition), you will find it helpful to have a Bible on hand for looking up other passages and cross-references or for comparing different translations.

The format of the guides in The Word Among Us Keys to the Bible series is especially well suited for use in small groups. Some recommendations and practical tips for using this guide in a Bible discussion group are offered on pages 110–113.

We hope that this guide will unlock the meaning of the Scriptures for you. May you grasp the full truth and reality of the life-giving power of the cross and share fully in the victory that Christ won for you.

The Word Among Us Press

Introduction

For Our Sake

For our sake he was crucified under Pontius Pilate;
he suffered, died, and was buried.
On the third day he rose again
  in fulfillment of the Scriptures;
he ascended into heaven
  and is seated at the right hand of the Father.
He will come again in glory
  to judge the living and the dead,
  and his kingdom will have no end.
—Nicene Creed

Every time we pray the Nicene Creed, we profess our faith in Jesus Christ and his saving deeds for us. These few sentences summarize the whole truth of our redemption. But the words have become so familiar that they trip off our tongues, almost without thought. We have memorized them and easily say them by heart, so to speak. But how deeply do we really understand their meaning? How can we truly grasp *by heart* the profound truths they contain?

In this guide, we will read and study Scripture texts that help us fathom Jesus' tremendous love as revealed through his passion, death, and resurrection. By studying the Scriptures about the meaning and power of the cross and prayerfully contemplating our crucified Lord, we will come to know the depths of his mercy and compassion toward us, sinners undeserving of such sacrificial love.

The Paradox of the Cross

"When mankind was estranged from him by disobedience, God our Savior made a plan for raising us from our fall and restoring us to friendship with himself," wrote St. Basil the Great in the fourth century. "According to this plan Christ came in the flesh, he showed us the gospel way of life, he suffered, died on the cross, was buried, and rose from the dead. He did this so that we could be saved by imitation of him, and recover our original status as sons of God by adoption."

In words echoing the Creed, Basil clearly and effectively reviews the history of humankind's redemption, the story of our need for salvation, and how God brought that about through his Son Jesus. Central to our salvation is Christ's death on the cross: Through his sacrifice, the Son of God conquered sin and Satan, overcame death's stranglehold on the human race, and restored us to union with our Creator. Jesus' cross is the greatest of paradoxes: Through his death we have received life. The cross may seem an instrument of torture in the eyes of unbelievers, but to those who do believe, it is the instrument of our salvation. "For the message about the cross is foolishness to those who are perishing, but to us who are being saved it is the power of God" (1 Corinthians 1:18).

St. Paul was the first to put into writing a "theology of the cross." In his letter to the church at Corinth, he explained, "In Christ God was reconciling the world to himself, not counting their trespasses against them. . . . For our sake he made him to be sin who knew no sin, so that in him we might become the righteousness of God" (2 Corinthians 5:19, 21). What good news it is that God reconciled the world to himself through Christ and does not count our sins and failings against us! But we are forgiven, not because God overlooked our trespasses, but because Christ took them upon himself. Reconciliation with God was won for us at the price of Jesus' death on the cross. His passion and crucifixion are a stark reminder that our salvation, forgiveness of our sin, is costly.

Not only does the cross bring us eternal life, but it also brings us a more abundant life here and now. Jesus "bore our sins in his body on the cross, so that, free from sins, we might live for righteousness" (1 Peter 2:24). His death on the cross won us victory over our sins—every one of them. Through his cross, Jesus has set us free from all that separates us from our Lord and prevents us from following him: our disobedience, our pride, our anger, and our self-centeredness. In Christ we die to this "old self," and in Christ we rise to the new.

Embraced by Christ's Love

In the first session of this guide, we will look at the evangelist John's eyewitness account of the historical event of Jesus' death. This text brings home to us the physical horror of the crucifixion, one of the most dreadful and excruciatingly painful forms of execution ever devised. Here we come face-to-face with Jesus' *passion*—that is, his burning love and passionate ardor for humankind and his fervent desire to save us—that led him to his passion on the cross. When we look to Golgotha, we see what love is. As Fr. Richard John Neuhaus once wrote, "The perfect self-surrender of the cross is, from eternity to eternity, at the heart of what it means to say that God is love." It is as if Jesus' arms are outstretched on the cross to take us into his loving embrace.

In the second session, we will meet the risen Lord and examine how his death was not simply a tragedy but also a triumph. Through dying on the cross and rising victoriously, Christ entered into his glory. Overcoming the curse of death that was upon us all, he opened the way for us to share glorious, eternal life with him and the Father.

The first two sessions include many references to texts from the ancient Hebrew Scriptures—the Christian Old Testament. As we study them, we will see that it was "in accordance with the scriptures" (1 Corinthians 15:3-4) that Jesus passed through all that he did for our sake. And as we come to recognize how Old Testament prophecies and "prefigurements" and "types" are fulfilled in Christ in the New Testament, we will grow in our understanding and appreciation of God and the marvelous plan of salvation his Son has carried out for us.

The Purpose and Power of the Cross

In the middle sessions (three to five), we will read and study selections mainly from the earliest of the New Testament writings, that is, from the letters of St. Paul and those of other first-century writers that unfolded for the fledgling Church an understanding of the purpose and power of the cross. Among the themes we will probe are how we have been redeemed by Christ's blood, how we have been reconciled with God and freed from slavery to sin and death by Christ's death, and how we ourselves have "died with Christ" to sin and live anew when we are "buried with him" in baptism (Romans 6:8, 4). As in the previous sessions, relevant passages from the Old Testament and the gospels that shed light on these topics are included.

Carrying the Cross as Christ's Disciples

Finally, the cross challenges every believer to discipleship. On several occasions Jesus told his uncomprehending disciples of his coming sufferings and death, and then immediately added, "If any want to become my followers, let them deny themselves and take up their cross and follow me" (Matthew 16:24). In his last public discourse, Jesus said to his listeners: "Those who love their life lose it, and those who hate their life in this world will keep it for eternal life. Whoever serves me must follow me, and where I am, there will my servant be also" (John 12:25-26).

The final session of this guide makes it clear that the cross marks the path that every disciple of Jesus is to follow. Called to take up Christ's cross, we can be confident that he who went the "way of the cross" before us will always be at our side to help us. Being a disciple, a follower of Christ, entails a costly emptying of self, but the privilege and joy of companionship with the One who spared nothing for our sake is our great reward.

Contemplating Christ's Passion and Resurrection

St. Thomas Aquinas once noted that "the Passion of Christ is enough to serve as a guide and model throughout our lives." But it is especially in the season of Lent that our thoughts and our hearts are turned to Christ's passion and crucifixion. Lent is a time for us to remember with gratitude Jesus' sacrifice—the price of our atonement paid for by his own blood. It is also a time for us to reflect on our need for this reconciliation, a time to ask how we have sinned or turned a deaf ear to God's call to us, and to repent.

Allow Paul's cry, "Be reconciled to God" (2 Corinthians 5:20), which we hear during the Ash Wednesday liturgy, to strike deeply at your heart. He persistently appeals to us not to reject God's offer of salvation, "not to accept the grace of God in vain" (6:1). "Now"—today, each and every day—"is the acceptable time" for us to return to the Lord, "now is the day of salvation" (6:2) for us. During the forty days of Lent, open your heart to the mystery of the cross and its meaning for you personally. Then, at the Easter Vigil, the night-watch of the resurrection, enter into the joy of Christ's victory as the Church sings its great proclamation, the *Exsultet*:

> This is the night when Christians everywhere,
> washed clean of sin
> and freed from all defilement,
> are restored to grace and grow together in holiness.
>
> This is the night when Jesus Christ
> broke the chains of death
> and rose triumphant from the grave. . . .
>
> Most blessed of all nights, chosen by God
> to see Christ rising from the dead!

Of this night scripture says:
"The night will be clear as day:
it will become my light, my joy."

The power of this holy night
dispels all evil, washes guilt away,
restores lost innocence, brings mourners joy;
it casts out hatred, brings us peace, and humbles
earthly pride.

Night truly blessed, when heaven is wedded to earth
and man is reconciled with God!

Let us take hold of the life-giving power of the cross so that we can share in the victory that Jesus won for us. Our hope is that on the last day, we will be united with him in his resurrection, healed and transformed in body, mind, and spirit, and wholly conformed to his image. "Now to him who by the power at work within us is able to accomplish abundantly far more than all we can ask or imagine, to him be glory in the church and in Christ Jesus to all generations, forever and ever. Amen" (Ephesians 3:20-21).

Jeanne Kun

"It Is Finished"

John 19:17-37

[17] Carrying the cross by himself, [Jesus] went out to what is called The Place of the Skull, which in Hebrew is called Golgotha. [18]There they crucified him, and with him two others, one on either side, with Jesus between them. [19]Pilate also had an inscription written and put on the cross. It read, "Jesus of Nazareth, the King of the Jews." [20]Many of the Jews read this inscription, because the place where Jesus was crucified was near the city; and it was written in Hebrew, in Latin, and in Greek. [21]Then the chief priests of the Jews said to Pilate, "Do not write, 'The King of the Jews,' but, 'This man said, I am King of the Jews.'" [22]Pilate answered, "What I have written I have written." [23]When the soldiers had crucified Jesus, they took his clothes and divided them into four parts, one for each soldier. They also took his tunic; now the tunic was seamless, woven in one piece from the top. [24]So they said to one another, "Let us not tear it, but cast lots for it to see who will get it." This was to fulfill what the scripture says,

> "They divided my clothes among themselves,
> and for my clothing they cast lots."

[25]And that is what the soldiers did.

Meanwhile, standing near the cross of Jesus were his mother, and his mother's sister, Mary the wife of Clopas, and Mary Magdalene. [26]When Jesus saw his mother and the disciple whom he loved standing beside her, he said to his mother, "Woman, here is your son." [27]Then he said to the disciple, "Here is your mother." And from that hour the disciple took her into his own home.

[28] After this, when Jesus knew that all was now finished, he said (in order to fulfill the scripture), "I am thirsty." [29]A jar full of sour wine was standing there. So they put a sponge full of the wine on a branch

> On the Cross the name of the Father is supremely "hallowed," and his Kingdom irrevocably comes; in the *"consummatum est"* his will is definitively done.
> —**Pope John Paul II,** *Letter to Priests,* Holy Thursday 1999

of hyssop and held it to his mouth. [30]When Jesus had received the wine, he said, "It is finished." Then he bowed his head and gave up his spirit.

[31] Since it was the day of Preparation, the Jews did not want the bodies left on the cross during the sabbath, especially because that sabbath was a day of great solemnity. So they asked Pilate to have the legs of the crucified men broken and the bodies removed. [32]Then the soldiers came and broke the legs of the first and of the other who had been crucified with him. [33]But when they came to Jesus and saw that he was already dead, they did not break his legs. [34]Instead, one of the soldiers pierced his side with a spear, and at once blood and water came out. [35](He who saw this has testified so that you also may believe. His testimony is true, and he knows that he tells the truth.) [36]These things occurred so that the scripture might be fulfilled, "None of his bones shall be broken." [37]And again another passage of scripture says, "They will look on the one whom they have pierced."

The evangelist John was an eyewitness to the events surrounding Jesus' crucifixion, and so we have a record of Jesus' last words: "It is finished" (John 19:30). On a literal level, these words signify the end of Jesus' life as he gave up his spirit to the Father. But they also express satisfaction—even triumph. In colloquial speech today, Jesus might have said, "Mission accomplished!"

God sent his Son into the world to heal the separation between God and humanity caused by the disobedience of Adam and Eve. Christ's crucifixion was not a failure of his mission or a meaningless waste of a good man's life cut off too soon but God's chosen means for our redemption: "God so loved the world that he gave his only Son, so that everyone who believes in him may not perish but may have eternal life." (John 3:16). And so by his death, Jesus' mission was completed. As Scripture scholar Jean-Pierre Prévost notes:

The Greek verb *tetelestai* means "brought to its accomplishment." Like he has done so many times, John uses here double entendre. The word "finished" refers to the physical and temporal end limit of Jesus' life. But it also tells, at the same time, about the total accomplishment of the mission entrusted to him by the Father.

After this declaration of his achievement, Jesus "bowed his head and gave up his spirit" (John 19:30). This "giving up" or "delivering over"—in Greek, *paradidomi*—is the same word used by St. Paul when he says that God "did not withhold his own Son, but *gave him up* for all of us" (Romans 8:32, emphasis added). Paul uses a similar phrase when referring to Christ: Jesus "gave himself up" (Ephesians 5:2, 25; see also Galatians 2:20), indicating that Jesus purposely delivered himself up to death for our sake.

> Christ's crucifixion was not a failure of his mission but God's chosen means for our redemption.

When Jesus breathed his last, he both handed his spirit back to the Father and handed on the Holy Spirit to the Church. The water that flowed from Jesus' pierced side symbolizes the Spirit made available to humanity because Jesus had now been glorified in the "lifting up" on the cross (John 19:34; 7:39; 12:32). His blood is a symbol of the redeeming work of the cross. Moreover, in this water and blood, the early Fathers of the Church saw allusions to the life-giving sacraments of Baptism and the Eucharist.

Also symbolic are Jesus' words to John, the "beloved disciple," who stood with Mary near enough to the cross to hear his dying master speak: "Woman, here is your son. . . . Here is your mother" (John 19:26-27). With these words Jesus created a new family: Mary received from Jesus a son in the beloved disciple—who represents each of us—and thus became the spiritual mother of all the faithful.

It is noteworthy that in Jesus' crucifixion we see the fulfillment of an important Jewish ritual, the annual Day of Atonement. On that day each year, the high priest entered into the inner tabernacle with an offering to atone for Israel's sins. On Golgotha Jesus was both the victim and the great high priest. The atoning sacrifice was no longer the blood of an animal but Jesus' own blood. No longer was it necessary for the high priest to enter into the Holy of Holies in the Jewish Temple, which was a symbol of the heavenly tabernacle. Now Jesus offered himself directly to his Father in heaven. The author of the Letter to the Hebrews points to Jesus' dual role as victim and priest:

> It was fitting that we should have such a high priest, holy, blameless, undefiled, separated from sinners, and exalted above the heavens. Unlike the other high priests, he has no need to offer sacrifices day after day, first for his own sins, and then for those of the people; this he did once for all when he offered himself. (Hebrews 7:26-27)

The twentieth-century Catholic apologist Frank Sheed explained the meaning and effect of Jesus' sacrificial death this way:

> What [Jesus] had become man to do was now done: expiation had been made, sufficient and overflowing for the first sin which had made the breach between God and the human race, and for all the sins by which the breach had been widened. This was atonement. Disguised by our pronunciation, the meaning of the word is at-one-ment. God and the human race had been at-two: now, and forever, they would be at one. Individual men might still separate themselves from God, but no one could separate the race of man. (*To Know Christ Jesus*)

Understand!

1. How well do you think Jesus' final words from the cross as recorded by John (19:30) summarize the purpose of his life—and death? Read Romans 3:23-25 and 2 Corinthians 5:17-18 to help you understand what Jesus "accomplished" on the cross, and then describe it in your own words.

   _____

   _____

   _____

   _____

   _____

   _____

2. Several times St. John refers to Scripture being "fulfilled" in the events on Golgotha: the casting of lots for Jesus' garments (John 19:23-24 and Exodus 28:32; Psalm 22:18); the fact that none of Jesus' bones were broken (John 19:36 and Exodus 12:46; Numbers 9:12; Psalm 34:20); observing the piercing of Jesus' side (John 19:37 and Zechariah 12:10). Why is it significant that these Old Testament prophecies were fulfilled? Why was it so important to John to preserve these details in his gospel?

   _____

   _____

   _____

   _____

   _____

   _____

3. What significance do you see in Jesus' words from the cross to Mary and John? What do these words, spoken even while he was suffering, reveal about Jesus' character? About his relationship with his mother and his disciple?

_____

_____

_____

_____

_____

4. John wrote: "He who saw this has testified so that you also may believe. His testimony is true, and he knows that he tells the truth" (John 19:35). Why did John stress so strongly that he was an eye-witness to the events surrounding Jesus' passion and death (see also 15:27 and 21:24)?

_____

_____

_____

_____

_____

5. Explain in your own words Jesus' dual role as victim and priest and how his death is an atonement. (You can look up the definition of "atonement" in a dictionary to enhance your understanding.)

_____

_____

_____

_____

_____

▶ In the Spotlight
Cry of Joy, Song of Triumph

"It is accomplished." *John 19:30*

It was not an utterance of thanksgiving that His suffering was over and finished, though the humiliation of the Son of Man was now at an end. It was rather that His life from the time of His birth to the time of His death had faithfully achieved what the Heavenly Father sent Him to do.

Three times God used that same word in history: first, in Genesis, to describe the achievement or completion of creation; second, in the Apocalypse, when all creation would be done away with and a new heaven and earth would be made. Between these two extremes of the beginning and the accomplished end, there was the link of the sixth utterance from the Cross. Our Divine Lord in the state of His greatest humiliation, seeing all prophecies fulfilled, all foreshadowings realized, and all things done which were for the Redemption of man, uttered a cry of joy: "It is achieved."

The life of the Spirit could now begin the work of sanctification, for the work of Redemption was completed. In creation, on the seventh day, after the heavens and the earth were finished, God rested from all the work that He had done; now the Savior on the Cross having taught as Teacher, governed as King, and sanctified as Priest, could enter into His rest. There would be no second Savior; no new way of salvation; no other name under heaven by which men might be saved. Man had been bought and paid for. A new David arose to slay the Goliath of evil, not with five stones but with five wounds—hideous scars on hands, feet, and side; and the battle was fought not with armor glistening under a noonday sun, but with flesh torn away so the bones could be numbered. The Artist had put the last touch on

his masterpiece, and with the joy of the strong He uttered the
song of triumph that His work was completed.
—**Fulton J. Sheen,** *Life of Christ*

Grow!

1. What is your response to the physical and emotional sufferings of
   Jesus? Which of the events surrounding Jesus' crucifixion or which
   of his words spoken from the cross makes the deepest impression
   on you? Why?

   _____

   _____

   _____

   _____

   _____

   _____

2. In your own words, paraphrase Jesus' final declaration, "It is finished." Describe a mission or task entrusted to you by God that
   you feel you have faithfully carried out or accomplished. What
   enabled you to do it?

   _____

   _____

   _____

   _____

   _____

   _____

3. In what ways has Jesus' accomplishment of his mission on the cross made a difference to you personally in restoring or healing your relationship with God? In what ways does this mission still need completion in your life?

_____

_____

_____

_____

_____

_____

4. In willingly giving himself over to death, Jesus paid an incredible price for our salvation. What does this reveal about his love for you? What could you do to concretely express your love for Jesus? To show your gratitude to him?

_____

_____

_____

_____

_____

_____

5. After Jesus' death, the beloved disciple "took [Mary] into his own home" (John 19:27). How have you made a place for Mary in your life and in your home? In what ways do you honor Mary as your spiritual mother? As the "Mother of the Church"?

_____

_____

_____

_____

_____

_____

▶ In the Spotlight
The Place of the Skull

Golgotha is the Greek transcription given by Matthew (27:33), Mark (15:22), and John (19:17) of the Aramaic word presumed to be *Gûlgaltâ* (אתלגלג) and explained by them to mean "skull." Luke simply calls the place in Greek *Kranion* ("cranium"), without giving the Aramaic form. The familiar English name "Calvary" comes from the Latin Vulgate translation of the Scripture by St. Jerome, which gives the Latin for "skull," *calvaria.*

The site used by the Romans for the public crucifixion of criminals is thought to have been an abandoned limestone quarry outside the western wall of Jerusalem, where a mound of unquarried rock jutted up twenty to thirty feet from the quarry floor. The place's name may have been derived from the physical contour of the rock, which possibly resembled a skull. Or, as some scholars propose, the site may have been called Golgotha because it was strewn with the skulls of those who had been executed there (this would have been contrary to Jewish burial traditions but not Roman ones) or in reference to a nearby cemetery (an idea consistent with the numerous tombs that have been found in the area by modern archaeologists). Later legends—influenced by the place-name and by Christian typology, which recognizes Jesus as the "new Adam" (Romans 5:14; 1 Corinthians 15:22, 45)—imaginatively consider the place of Christ's crucifixion to also be the burial place of Adam's skull.

Gospel accounts indicate that the site of Jesus' crucifixion was outside the walls of Jerusalem. Most likely it was near a road where it would have been easily seen by those entering and leaving the city through the gate of Ephraim, because public execution was intended to be not only a punishment of criminals but a warning to others to avoid the same fate by avoiding their crimes. In A.D. 326 the Roman emperor Constantine had a large basilica built over this site, and today what remains of the rock of Golgotha is venerated under an altar in the present Church of the Holy Sepulchre. Modern archaeological excavations have established that this site was indeed outside the so-called second north wall of Jerusalem and the gate of Ephraim in the first century.

Reflect!

1. Read Genesis 22:1-19. As the commentary in *The Navarre Bible* states,

> The sacrifice of Isaac has features which make it a figure of the redemptive sacrifice of Christ. Thus, there is the father giving up his son; the son who surrenders himself to his father's will; and the tools of sacrifice such as the wood, the knife and the altar. The account reaches its climax by showing that through Abraham's obedience and Isaac's non-resistance, God's blessing will reach all the nations of the earth (cf. v. 18). So, it is not surprising that Jewish tradition should attribute a certain redemptive value to Isaac's submissiveness, and that the Fathers should see this episode as prefiguring the passion of Christ, the only Son of the Father.

What does this mysterious and painful story add to your understanding of God, the Father "who did not withhold [*spare*, RSV] his own Son, but gave him up for all of us" (Romans 8:32)?

2. Reflect on the following passages to enhance your understanding of the cross as an expression of the depth of Christ's love for you and as a fulfillment of the Father's plan for your salvation:

> He had no form or majesty that we should look at him, nothing in his appearance that we should desire him.

He was despised and rejected by others;
  a man of suffering and acquainted with infirmity;
and as one from whom others hide their faces
  he was despised, and we held him of no account.

Surely he has borne our infirmities
  and carried our diseases;
yet we accounted him stricken,
  struck down by God, and afflicted.
But he was wounded for our transgressions,
  crushed for our iniquities;
upon him was the punishment that made us whole,
  and by his bruises we are healed.
All we like sheep have gone astray;
  we have all turned to our own way,
and the LORD has laid on him
  the iniquity of us all. (Isaiah 53:2-6)

[Jesus said:] "For this reason the Father loves me, because I lay down my life in order to take it up again. No one takes it from me, but I lay it down of my own accord. I have power to lay it down, and I have power to take it up again. I have received this command from my Father." (John 10:17-18)

Though he was in the form of God,
  [Christ Jesus] did not regard equality with God
  as something to be exploited,
but emptied himself,
  taking the form of a slave,
  being born in human likeness.
And being found in human form,
  he humbled himself

and became obedient to the point of death—
even death on a cross. (Philippians 2:6-8)

He himself bore our sins in his body on the cross, so that,
free from sins, we might live for righteousness; by his
wounds you have been healed. For you were going astray
like sheep, but now you have returned to the shepherd and
guardian of your souls. (1 Peter 2:24-25)

▶ In the Spotlight
In the Words of the Saints

Where have your love, your mercy, your compassion shone out
more luminously than in your wounds, sweet gentle Lord of
mercy? More mercy than this no one has than that he lay down
his life for those who are doomed to death.
—St. Bernard of Clairvaux

Yes, my sweet Savior, I see you all covered with wounds. I look
into your beautiful face but, O my God, it no longer wears its
beautiful appearance. It is disfigured and blackened with blood
and bruises, and shameful spittings: *He had no form or comeli-*
ness that we should look at him, and no beauty that we should
desire him (Isaiah 53:2). But the more I see you so disfigured,
O my Lord, the more beautiful and lovely you appear to me.
And what are these disfigurements but signs of the tenderness
of that love you have for me?
—St. Alphonsus Liguori

> Look at the Cross and you will see Jesus' head bent to kiss you,
> His arms extended to embrace you, His heart opened to receive
> you, to enclose you within His love.
> —Blessed Teresa of Calcutta

Act!

St. Thérèse of Lisieux, known in her Carmelite monastery as Sr. Thérèse of the Child Jesus and of the Holy Face, once wrote to her sister Céline about the crucified Lord: "Jesus is on fire with love for us.... Look at his adorable face! ... Look at his eyes lifeless and lowered! Look at his wounds.... Look at Jesus in his face.... There you will see how he loves us" (Letter 87).

Kneel before a crucifix or sit quietly before an image of the suffering Christ and follow Thérèse's exhortation to look at Jesus' face and at his wounds. Meditate on Jesus' great love for you, and then express to him your love and your gratitude that he died for your sake and for the sake of all humankind.

▶ In the Spotlight
"The Passion of Jesus Is an Ocean of Love"

> Throughout his life, Paul Daneo (1694–1775) was so consumed with a single-hearted devotion to the crucified Christ that he is now known as St. Paul of the Cross. At the foot of the cross, through Christ's sacrificial love, Paul found that humankind's suffering was transformed and death was overcome.
>
> Even as a youth, Paul was moved by the sufferings of Jesus and developed a deep love for the crucified Lord. When he was

twenty-six, the Blessed Mother appeared to him. Garbed in a black robe with a white emblem bearing Christ's name and a cross, Mary directed him to establish a new religious order dedicated to her Son's passion. Seven years later, in 1727, Paul was ordained, and together with his brother and his best friend founded the Congregation of the Passionists. At their profession members of the congregation take a habit with the emblem that Paul saw in his vision of Mary and add to the three customary religious vows of poverty, chastity, and obedience a fourth—to promote devotion to the passion of the Lord.

The Passionists rapidly became known throughout Italy for their parish missions and retreats. Paul was especially renowned as a preacher, stirring the crowds to conversion and repentance with his message of God's love and mercy as revealed on the cross. "The passion of Jesus is a sea of sorrows, but it is also an ocean of love," he frequently declared. "Ask the Lord to teach you to fish in this ocean. Dive into its depths. No matter how deep you go, you will never reach the bottom."

Paul Daneo died in 1775 and was canonized by Pope Pius IX in 1867. Today the Congregation of the Passionists continues to carry on the mission of St. Paul of the Cross throughout the world with this inspiring message: Join yourself spiritually with Christ in his death so as to rise up with him to a life of faith and love.

"The Lord Has Risen Indeed"

Luke 24:13-47

¹³ Now on that same day two of them were going to a village called Emmaus, about seven miles from Jerusalem, ¹⁴and talking with each other about all these things that had happened. ¹⁵While they were talking and discussing, Jesus himself came near and went with them, ¹⁶but their eyes were kept from recognizing him. ¹⁷And he said to them, "What are you discussing with each other while you walk along?" They stood still, looking sad. ¹⁸Then one of them, whose name was Cleopas, answered him, "Are you the only stranger in Jerusalem who does not know the things that have taken place there in these days?" ¹⁹He asked them, "What things?" They replied, "The things about Jesus of Nazareth, who was a prophet mighty in deed and word before God and all the people, ²⁰and how our chief priests and leaders handed him over to be condemned to death and crucified him. ²¹But we had hoped that he was the one to redeem Israel. Yes, and besides all this, it is now the third day since these things took place. ²²Moreover, some women of our group astounded us. They were at the tomb early this morning, ²³and when they did not find his body there, they came back and told us that they had indeed seen a vision of angels who said that he was alive. ²⁴Some of those who were with us went to the tomb and found it just as the women had said; but they did not see him." ²⁵Then he said to them, "Oh, how foolish you are, and how slow of heart to believe all that the prophets have declared! ²⁶Was it not necessary that the Messiah should suffer these things and then enter into his glory?" ²⁷Then beginning with Moses and all the prophets, he interpreted to them the things about himself in all the scriptures.

²⁸ As they came near the village to which they were going, he walked ahead as if he were going on. ²⁹But they urged him strongly, saying,

> When Death and Life contended,
> the Lord of life was slain.
> A battle strangely ended:
> he won, and lives to reign.
> —**Easter Sequence,**
> *Victimae Paschali Laudes*

"Stay with us, because it is almost evening and the day is now nearly over." So he went in to stay with them. ³⁰When he was at table with them, he took bread, blessed and broke it, and gave it to them. ³¹Then their eyes were opened, and they recognized him; and he vanished from their sight. ³²They said to each other, "Were not our hearts burning within us while he was talking to us on the road, while he was opening the scriptures to us?" ³³That same hour they got up and returned to Jerusalem; and they found the eleven and their companions gathered together. ³⁴They were saying, "The Lord has risen indeed, and he has appeared to Simon!" ³⁵Then they told what had happened on the road, and how he had been made known to them in the breaking of the bread.

³⁶ While they were talking about this, Jesus himself stood among them and said to them, "Peace be with you." ³⁷They were startled and terrified, and thought that they were seeing a ghost. ³⁸He said to them, "Why are you frightened, and why do doubts arise in your hearts? ³⁹Look at my hands and my feet; see that it is I myself. Touch me and see; for a ghost does not have flesh and bones as you see that I have." ⁴⁰And when he had said this, he showed them his hands and his feet. ⁴¹While in their joy they were disbelieving and still wondering, he said to them, "Have you anything here to eat?" ⁴²They gave him a piece of broiled fish, ⁴³and he took it and ate in their presence.

⁴⁴ Then he said to them, "These are my words that I spoke to you while I was still with you—that everything written about me in the law of Moses, the prophets, and the psalms must be fulfilled." ⁴⁵Then he opened their minds to understand the scriptures, ⁴⁶and he said to them, "Thus it is written, that the Messiah is to suffer and to rise from the dead on the third day, ⁴⁷and that repentance and forgiveness of sins is to be proclaimed in his name to all nations, beginning from Jerusalem."

Was it not necessary that the Messiah should suffer these things and then enter into his glory?" (Luke 24:26). The key to understanding Jesus' mission to save and restore humanity to union with the Father is found in this question and the explanation Jesus gave to his bewildered followers. As he opened the Scriptures to them (24:27), he showed that it was by his crucifixion that he fulfilled his Father's plan for the salvation of the world. Christians can now look upon the cross not as a shameful instrument of torture but as a sign of victory. Jesus' crucifixion was a battle that ultimately delivered all humankind from the power of Satan—from sin and from death. And we, who are in Christ, share in this victory.

Jesus went to his death on Golgotha knowing that it was the path to his glorification as well as our salvation. In his last public discourse, he had indicated how—and why—he would soon die, saying, "Now my soul is troubled. And what should I say—'Father, save me from this hour'? No, it is for this reason that I have come to this hour. Father, glorify your name. . . . And I, when I am lifted up from the earth, will draw all people to myself" (John 12:27-28, 32). And on the very eve of his crucifixion, Jesus prayed:

> Father, the hour has come; glorify your Son so that the Son may glorify you, since you have given him authority over all people, to give eternal life to all whom you have given him. And this is eternal life, that they may know you, the only true God, and Jesus Christ whom you have sent. I glorified you on earth by finishing the work that you gave me to do. So now, Father, glorify me in your own presence with the glory that I had in your presence before the world existed. (John 17:1-5)

The Fathers of the Church even refer to the cross as Jesus' "throne of glory." The crucifixion led ultimately to Jesus' resurrection and ascension into heaven, where he is gloriously enthroned at the right hand of the Father (Hebrews 1:3).

Jesus showed his followers the wounds in his hands and feet and side to assure them that his resurrected body was the same body that had been crucified (Luke 24:39-40; John 20:27). As the *Catechism of the Catholic Church* explains, "[Jesus'] authentic, real body possesses the new properties of a glorious body: not limited by space and time but able to be present how and when he wills; for Christ's humanity can no longer be confined to earth and belongs henceforth only to the Father's divine realm" (645). When death entered the world through sin, we lost sight of our immortality and our heavenly destiny. But because of Christ's passion and glorification, we can anticipate with joy that, after death, our own perishable, physical bodies will be raised up and vested with unimaginable splendor. And even now, "He who raised Christ from the dead will give life to [our] mortal bodies also through his Spirit that dwells in [us]" (Romans 8:11). Day by day the risen Lord brings healing, freedom, and transformation to us and produces the fruits of the Spirit in us; ultimately, in our imperishable bodies, we will share eternal glory with Jesus and the Father in heaven.

> Jesus went to his death on Golgotha knowing that it was the path to his glorification as well as our salvation.

It is awesome to realize that Jesus retains the marks of his wounds on his resurrected body. They are a badge of his sufferings, like the battle scars proudly worn by a veteran. As Pope Benedict XVI has noted, "The Lord took his wounds with him to eternity. He is a wounded God. . . . His wounds are a sign for us that he understands and allows himself to be wounded out of love for us." The scars of Jesus' crucifixion are the sign of the price he willingly paid with his own body for our redemption, the mark of his passionate love for us.

When the risen Lord appeared to the eleven, he said to them: "'Everything written about me in the law of Moses, the prophets, and the psalms must be fulfilled.' Then he opened their minds to understand the scriptures, and said to them, 'Thus it is written, that the Messiah is to suffer and to rise from the dead on the third day'" (Luke 24:44-46). From its earliest days, the Church recognized the significance of Christ's fulfillment of prophecy; its faith in Jesus the Messiah was rooted in God's word. As St. Paul attested, "I handed on to you as of first importance what I in turn had received: that Christ died for our sins in accordance with the scriptures, and that he was buried, and that he was raised on the third day in accordance with the scriptures" (1 Corinthians 15:3-4).

Understand!

1. Luke reports that Cleopas and his companion failed to recognize Jesus when he joined them on the road (24:16). What do you think might account for this failure? Do you think the appearance of Jesus' resurrected body was a factor? Why or why not?

_____

_____

_____

_____

_____

_____

2. How did the two travelers describe Jesus of Nazareth to their unknown companion (Luke 24:19-24)? What were their beliefs about Jesus and their expectations of him before he had been crucified? Why were they so disappointed? Why do you think the two were so "slow of heart" (24:25) to believe?

_____

_____

_____

_____

_____

3. What did Jesus stress in his explanation of the Scriptures concerning himself to his followers (Luke 24:25-27, 44-46)? What does this indicate to you about how the early Church viewed the ancient prophecies of the Hebrew Scriptures as it formed its understanding of Christ?

_____

_____

_____

_____

_____

_____

4. How did the travelers react to Jesus? Describe the process of their recognition of Jesus and the effect of his explanation of the Scriptures upon them. What does this suggest to you about the power of the word of God? About Jesus' physical appearance? About his spiritual "presence" and charisma?

_____

_____

_____

_____

_____

_____

5. Since his death on the cross, how has Jesus drawn all people to himself, as he promised (John 12:32)? How is this connected to his glorification?

_____

_____

_____

_____

_____

_____

▶ In the Spotlight
The Witness of the Early Church

If you would understand that the cross is Christ's triumph, hear what he himself also said: "When I am lifted up, then I will draw all men to myself." Now you can see that the cross is Christ's glory and triumph.
—St. Andrew of Crete

No one, however weak, is denied a share in the victory of the cross. No one is beyond the help of the prayer of Christ. His prayer brought benefit to the multitude that raged against him. How much more does it bring to those who turn to him in repentance.
—St. Leo the Great

Glory be to you, O Christ, who laid your cross as a bridge over death, that souls might pass over it from the dwelling of the dead to the dwelling of life!
—St. Ephrem of Syria

Grow!

1. Like the two disciples on the road to Emmaus, have you ever failed to recognize Jesus' presence or action in your life or felt downcast and disappointed, without hope for your future? What were your prayers to Jesus like then? How did the Lord reveal himself to you and encourage you?

_____

_____

_____

_____

_____

2. How has your knowledge of Old Testament prophecies that were fulfilled in Jesus deepened your faith? What particular word of Scripture has caused your heart to "burn" within you? Why?

_____

_____

_____

_____

_____

_____

3. Recall an instance in your life when you experienced "glory" or "victorious new life" coming out of suffering or what seemed like failure and defeat. What did you learn about God and his redemptive power from this circumstance?

_____

_____

_____

_____

_____

4. How does your personal faith in Jesus' resurrection and the future resurrection of the dead affect your outlook toward those around you—mortal men and women who, along with you, will "put on immortality" (1 Corinthians 15:53) and live eternally? How does it affect your feelings about your own death?

_____

_____

_____

_____

_____

_____

5. How do you envision Jesus' glorified body (Luke 24:36-40; John 20:19-20; Revelation 1:12-16)? How do you imagine your own resurrected existence in heaven?

_____

_____

_____

_____

_____

_____

▶ In the Spotlight
So Must the Son of Man Be Lifted Up

In his nighttime conversation with Nicodemus (John 3:1-15), Jesus prophetically alluded to his "lifting up" and glorification on the cross: "Just as Moses lifted up the serpent in the wilderness, so must the Son of Man be lifted up, that whoever believes in him may have eternal life" (3:14-15). The story of the Israelites' rebellion against God in Numbers 21:5-9 gives us insight into how we are to understand Jesus' mysterious statement:

The people spoke against God and against Moses, "Why have you brought us up out of Egypt to die in the wilderness? For there is no food and no water, and we detest this miserable food." Then the LORD sent poisonous serpents among the people, and they bit the people, so that many Israelites died. The people came to Moses and said, "We have sinned by speaking against the LORD and against you; pray to the LORD to take away the serpents from us." So Moses prayed for the people. And the LORD said to Moses, "Make a poisonous serpent, and set it on a pole; and everyone who is bitten shall look at it and live." So

Moses made a serpent of bronze, and put it upon a pole; and whenever a serpent bit someone, that person would look at the serpent of bronze and live.

The bronze serpent is a "type" or prefigurement of Christ. By looking at the image erected on the pole by Moses, those who had sinned and been bitten by the venomous serpents were cured. Jesus compares this incident with his coming crucifixion to show the purpose of his being raised up on the cross: Anyone who looks on him with faith can obtain salvation, for the cross is God's remedy or antidote for the sting of Satan and the poisonous venom of sin that infects humanity. As Benedictine monk and Scripture scholar Damasus Winzen wrote, "The fiery serpents are the symbol of the sins of men, and the bronze serpent foreshadows the one who took on the flesh of sins without sin, that through faith in his death for our sins, we may be freed from death" (*Pathways in Scripture*).

Reflect!

1. When we say the Apostles' Creed, we proclaim our faith in Jesus' resurrection and in "the resurrection of the body"—that is, in our own future resurrection. Although we cannot comprehend now how our bodies of flesh will be transformed, we know that "the dead will be raised imperishable, and we will be changed. . . . When this perishable body puts on imperishability, and this mortal body puts on immortality, then the saying that is written will be fulfilled: 'Death has been swallowed up in victory'" (1 Corinthians 15:52, 54).

How do you show respect for your physical body, which is destined for immortality? How might reflection on your own future resurrected body affect what you do in daily life?

2. Read and reflect on the following Scripture passages to deepen your appreciation of the victorious nature of Christ's resurrection and the eternal life that the faithful will come to share with him in heaven:

> A week later [Jesus'] disciples were again in the house, and Thomas was with them. Although the doors were shut, Jesus came and stood among them and said, "Peace be with you." Then he said to Thomas, "Put your finger here and see my hands. Reach out your hand and put it in my side. Do not doubt but believe." Thomas answered him, "My Lord and my God!" (John 20:26-28)

> Now if Christ is proclaimed as raised from the dead, how can some of you say there is no resurrection of the dead? If there is no resurrection of the dead, then Christ has not been raised; and if Christ has not been raised, then our proclamation has been in vain and your faith has been in vain. We are even found to be misrepresenting God, because we testified of God that he raised Christ—whom he did not raise if it is true that the dead are not raised. For if the dead are not raised, then Christ has not been raised. If Christ has not been raised, your faith is futile and you are still in your sins. Then those also who have died in Christ have perished. If for this life only we have hoped in Christ, we are of all people most to be pitied.
>
> But in fact Christ has been raised from the dead, the first fruits of those who have died. For since death came through a human being, the resurrection of the dead has also come through a human being; for as all die in Adam, so all will be made alive in Christ. (1 Corinthians 15:12-22)

> For since we believe that Jesus died and rose again, even so, through Jesus, God will bring with him those who have

died. For this we declare to you by the word of the Lord, that we who are alive, who are left until the coming of the Lord, will by no means precede those who have died. For the Lord himself, with a cry of command, with the archangel's call and with the sound of God's trumpet, will descend from heaven, and the dead in Christ will rise first. Then we who are alive, who are left, will be caught up in the clouds together with them to meet the Lord in the air; and so we will be with the Lord forever. Therefore encourage one another with these words. (1 Thessalonians 4:14-18)

▶ In the Spotlight
The Throne of Love

The chief priests of Jesus' own people accused him of falsely claiming to be a king (Luke 23:2). Ironically, it was the gentile Pilate who, defying the Jewish elders, ordered that the title "Jesus of Nazareth, the King of the Jews" be affixed to the cross when Jesus was crucified (John 19:19-22). In the Tradition and writings of the Church, Jesus' crucifixion is frequently called his "enthronement"—an expression of kingship—because the cross, the instrument of his death, was also recognized as the means of his glorification and a sign of his victorious reign.

The throne of this King whom we worship . . . is the Cross, and his triumph is the victory of Love, an almighty love that from the Cross pours out his gifts upon humanity of all times and all places.
—**Pope Benedict XVI**

We venerate the cross as a safeguard of faith, as the strengthening of hope and the throne of love. It is the sign of mercy, the proof of forgiveness, the vehicle of grace and the banner of peace. We venerate the cross, because it has broken down our pride, shattered our envy, redeemed our sin, and atoned for our punishment. . . .

Whatever we accomplish for God, whatever we succeed and hope for, is the fruit of our veneration of the cross. By the cross Christ draws everything to him. It is the kingdom of the Father, the scepter of the Son and the seal of the Holy Spirit, a witness to the total Trinity.

—**Rupert of Deutz**

Act!

This week share your faith in Christ's resurrection with someone you know who is facing challenging circumstances (for example, physical illness, a financial crisis, depression, or a sense of hopelessness). Encourage this person to hold fast to the eternal perspective that St. Paul offers in Romans 8:18-19 and 22-25:

I consider that the sufferings of this present time are not worth comparing with the glory about to be revealed to us. For the creation waits with eager longing for the revealing of the children of God. . . . We know that the whole creation has been groaning in labor pains until now; and not only the creation, but we ourselves, who have the first fruits of the Spirit, groan inwardly while we wait for adoption, the redemption of our bodies. For in hope we were saved. Now hope that is seen is not hope. For who hopes for what is seen? But if we hope for what we do not see, we wait for it with patience.

▶ In the Spotlight
The Exaltation of the Holy Cross

Though the ancient world shuddered at the thought of death by crucifixion—a horrific and shameful form of execution—Christians recognize Jesus' cross as both the sign of his suffering and the trophy of his victory over Satan, sin, and death. We revere the cross because through it we have come to know Jesus' great love for us, and through the wounds that it inflicted, we have been saved and healed. This instrument of cruelty and disgrace is now honored as God's instrument of triumph and glory, especially in the Feast of the Exaltation of the Holy Cross, which has a long history in the Church.

In 326 the mother of the emperor Constantine, St. Helena, led excavators to the place where a cross believed to be Christ's was discovered. This discovery was first celebrated on September 14 in 365 in the church that Constantine built over the site of Golgotha and the tomb of Jesus. The observance of the "finding of the cross" spread quickly among Christians throughout the world. The commemoration of this event was later coupled with a feast commemorating the emperor Heraclius' victory in 629 over Chosroes, King of Persia—a victory that restored to the Christian world the precious relic of the true cross that had been seized by the Persians. Today the feast, which recalls both historical events, is known in the Roman calendar as the Feast of the Exaltation, or Triumph, of the Holy Cross and is still celebrated on September 14.

"This Cup . . . Is the New Covenant"

Exodus 24:3-8

24:3Moses came and told the people all the words of the LORD and all the ordinances; and all the people answered with one voice, and said, "All the words that the LORD has spoken we will do." 4And Moses wrote down all the words of the LORD. He rose early in the morning and built an altar at the foot of the mountain, and set up twelve pillars, corresponding to the twelve tribes of Israel. 5He sent young men of the people of Israel, who offered burnt offerings and sacrificed oxen as offerings of well-being to the LORD. 6Moses took half of the blood and put it in basins, and half of the blood he dashed against the altar. 7Then he took the book of the covenant, and read it in the hearing of the people; and they said, "All that the LORD has spoken we will do, and we will be obedient." 8Moses took the blood and dashed it on the people, and said, "See the blood of the covenant that the LORD has made with you in accordance with all these words."

> Let us fix our eyes on the blood of Christ and realize how precious it is to the Father, seeing that it was poured out for our salvation and brought the grace of conversion to the whole world.
> —Pope St. Clement I

Luke 22:14, 19-20

14 When the hour came, [Jesus] took his place at the table, and the apostles with him. . . . 19Then he took a loaf of bread, and when he had given thanks, he broke it and gave it to them, saying, "This is my body, which is given for you. Do this in remembrance of me." 20And he did the same with the cup after supper, saying, "This cup that is poured out for you is the new covenant of my blood." (See also Matthew 26:19-20, 26-28 and Mark 14:16-17, 22-24)

Hebrews 9:11-22

11 When Christ came as a high priest of the good things that have come, then through the greater and perfect tent (not made with hands, that is, not of this creation), 12he entered once for all into the Holy Place, not with the blood of goats and calves, but with his own blood, thus obtaining eternal redemption. 13For if the blood of goats and bulls, with the sprinkling of the ashes of a heifer, sanctifies those who have been defiled so that their flesh is purified, 14how much more will the blood of Christ, who through the eternal Spirit offered himself without blemish to God, purify our conscience from dead works to worship the living God!

15 For this reason he is the mediator of a new covenant, so that those who are called may receive the promised eternal inheritance, because a death has occurred that redeems them from the transgressions under the first covenant. 16Where a will is involved, the death of the one who made it must be established. 17For a will takes effect only at death, since it is not in force as long as the one who made it is alive. 18Hence not even the first covenant was inaugurated without blood. 19For when every commandment had been told to all the people by Moses in accordance with the law, he took the blood of calves and goats, with water and scarlet wool and hyssop, and sprinkled both the scroll itself and all the people, 20saying, "This is the blood of the covenant that God has ordained for you." 21And in the same way he sprinkled with the blood both the tent and all the vessels used in worship. 22Indeed, under the law almost everything is purified with blood, and without the shedding of blood there is no forgiveness of sins.

Why—and how—is it that Jesus "obtained eternal redemption" (Hebrews 9:12) for us through the shedding of his blood on the cross?

No human or animal life can be sustained without blood circulating through the body. The ancient Israelites considered blood sacred because they recognized that life depends on it: "For the life of every creature—its blood is its life" (Leviticus 17:14). Because blood is a vital life force and so sacred, a blood offering was therefore the highest form of sacrifice and could make atonement for sin: "For the life of the flesh is in the blood; and I have given it to you for making atonement for your lives on the altar" (17:11; see also 16:11-19). The blood of the animal sacrifice was a substitution for the blood of the one making the offering; the blood of the sacrifice was poured out to acknowledge the penalty due for sin.

The Israelites also recognized that blood purifies and cleanses. As the author of Hebrews explains, "When every commandment had been told to all the people by Moses in accordance with the law, he took the blood of lambs and goats . . . and sprinkled both the scroll itself and all the people. . . . Indeed, under the law almost everything is purified with blood, and without the shedding of blood there is no forgiveness of sins" (9:19, 22). Thus, when the Israelites ratified the covenant at Mount Sinai with the sprinkling of blood, they were not only pledging their lives and their obedience to God but were also being cleansed of their transgressions and wrongdoing.

The words that Moses spoke at Sinai—"See the blood of the covenant that the LORD has made with you" (Exodus 24:8)—foreshadowed Jesus' own words at the Last Supper: "This cup that is poured out for you is the new covenant in my blood" (Luke 22:20; see also Matthew 26:28). In the sacrifice of the Eucharist instituted on the eve before his death and the sacrifice of Calvary, Jesus himself—not a bull or lamb—was the sacrificial victim whose lifeblood was offered as the atonement for our sins. Through his sacrifice, he sealed with us a new covenant, the covenant of our redemption. Furthermore, as the great Church father St. John Chrysostom so eloquently wrote, "This Blood, poured out in abundance, has washed the whole world clean."

> By offering his lifeblood, Christ became the mediator of a new covenant—the covenant of our redemption.

At Sinai, Moses served as the mediator between God and the Israelite people. At the Last Supper and on Calvary, by offering his lifeblood, Christ became "the mediator of a new covenant"—and thus established a new relationship between God and his people. Again the author of Hebrews helps us understand why Jesus' death was necessary by explaining that the Greek word for "covenant" can also mean "last will and testament" and that "a will takes effect only at death, since it is not in force as long as the one who made it is alive." When Jesus died on the cross, his last will "took effect"; consequently, we can receive "the promised eternal inheritance" (Hebrews 9:15-17).

Christ's offering of himself is the greatest and costliest offering ever made to God: We have been ransomed from sin, "not with perishable things like silver or gold, but with the precious blood of Christ, like that of a lamb without defect or blemish" (1 Peter 1:18-19). Moreover, Jesus' self-offering never has to be repeated—"Unlike the other high priests, he has no need to offer sacrifices day after day, first for his own sins, and then for those of the people; this he did once for all when he offered himself" (Hebrews 7:27). Yet it is also true that in every celebration of the Mass, the sacrifice Jesus offered on Calvary remains present to us: "In this divine sacrifice which is celebrated in the Mass, the same Christ who offered himself once in a bloody manner on the altar of the cross is contained and is offered in an unbloody manner" (Council of Trent). When we receive the Eucharist, we become participants in Jesus' sacrifice and partakers in the gift of salvation.

When Pilate could not outmaneuver the religious leaders who were demanding that Jesus be crucified and convince them that Jesus should be released, he "washed his hands before the crowd, saying, 'I am innocent of this man's blood; see to it yourselves.' Then the people as a whole answered, 'His blood be on us and on our children!'" (Matthew 27:24-25). Little did they realize the true significance of their words, for it is through the atoning death of Jesus that sin-ridden humankind has been reconciled to God. Through the shedding of his blood, Jesus has removed our condemnation and forgiven our wrongdoing. Here and now we can stand before God with confidence, cleansed of our guilty conscience, free from fear of punishment. We can place our faith in the blood of Christ even now to heal us and free us. And we can look forward to sharing eternal life with Jesus and the Father.

Understand!

1. When Moses "dashed against the altar" the blood of the animal sacrifice, what did the Israelites understand this action to symbolize? (Exodus 24:6). Why was the blood also sprinkled on the people (24:8)?

   _____

   _____

   _____

   _____

   _____

   _____

2. According to Jesus' own words at the Last Supper, for what purpose did he offer his blood (see Matthew 26:28 as well as Luke 22:20)? Which verses in particular in Hebrews 9:11-22 point to the same purpose?

_____

_____

_____

_____

_____

_____

3. Explain in your own words how Jesus' "last will" took effect, and describe the inheritance you have received through it.

_____

_____

_____

_____

_____

_____

4. What are the chief role and function of a mediator? (You can look up the definition of "mediator" in a dictionary to enhance your understanding.) What did Jesus accomplish as a mediator? Between whom did he mediate? Why was his mediation necessary?

_____

_____

_____

_____

_____

_____

5. What similarities do you see between the sacrifices offered by the priests of ancient Israel and Jesus' sacrifice of himself? In what ways do they differ, and how is this significant?

_____

_____

_____

_____

_____

_____

▶ In the Spotlight
Wisdom from the Doctors of the Church

Drink Christ because he is the river whose current gladdens the city of God; drink Christ because he is peace; drink Christ because from his side flow living waters; drink Christ to drink the blood which redeemed you; drink Christ to drink his words.
—**St. Ambrose**

On the cross Christ effected a great exchange. There the purse containing the price to be paid for us was opened. When the soldier's lance cut its way into his side, the price paid for the whole world flowed forth.
—**St. Augustine**

Remain in the holy and sweet love of God. Drown yourself in the Blood of Christ crucified; put yourself on the Cross with Christ crucified; hide yourself in the Wounds of Christ crucified; bathe yourself in the Blood of Christ crucified.
—**St. Catherine of Siena**

> I adore you, O precious blood of Jesus. . . . I place my trust in you, O adorable blood, our redemption, our regeneration. Fall, drop by drop, into the hearts that have wandered from you and soften their hardness.
> —**St. Albert the Great**

Grow!

1. How could someone who does not believe in Jesus tell from your life that you have been redeemed by the blood of Jesus? What are some ways you might respond differently to life's trials and temptations than someone who does not know Jesus?

   _____

   _____

   _____

   _____

   _____

   _____

2. How do you feel when you think of Christ physically shedding his blood for you? When in your life have you made a sacrifice that was so great that it felt like it cost you your "blood"? How did you feel about it afterward?

   _____

   _____

   _____

   _____

   _____

   _____

3. What insights does the Israelites' ritual sealing of the covenant at Sinai give you into the nature of the Eucharist as a sacrifice? As a covenant sign? How do you actively participate in the new covenant that God made through Christ? What does God ask of you in your covenant relationship with him?

_____

_____

_____

_____

_____

_____

4. Pope Benedict XVI has called the Eucharist "the Sacrament in which the whole work of Redemption is concentrated." What fruits of redemption have you experienced through receiving Christ's body and blood in Communion? In what ways have you been transformed or healed by your reception of this sacrament?

_____

_____

_____

_____

_____

_____

5. How do you prepare yourself to receive Communion? If you approach the sacrament in a somewhat casual or merely routine manner, what could you do to foster greater reverence for Christ present in the Eucharist? What response do you make to Christ for the gift of the Eucharist?

_____

_____

_____

_____

_____

▶ In the Spotlight
Faith in the Blood of Christ

When we talk about "sprinkling" the blood of Jesus over us, we are not talking about a physical sprinkling, but about placing our faith in the blood that Jesus shed and in its power in our lives. . . . Praying with faith in Jesus' blood is powerful. It can change our lives—not because of the words we speak, but because of the mercy of God. . . .

Julie is the mother of three children. Fourteen yeas ago, and for reasons she still can't understand, her husband walked out on her and the family. Every night Julie went to bed plagued by misery and guilt. She cried every day and was afraid she didn't have the strength to raise her children alone. She felt like a failure, but she didn't know where she had gone wrong. All she knew was that she wanted her husband to come home.

When a friend from church told Julie about Jesus' blood and taught her how to pray the blood of Jesus over her heart and mind, things began to change. Her husband never came home, but she gradually was freed from the sense of guilt and failure that had paralyzed her and dragged her down. She knew Jesus was with her, and she began to take control over her situation. If you were to meet Julie's family today, you'd be very impressed by her sense of peace and the way her children have grown up. She herself says that she is a living testimony to the healing power of the blood of Christ.

—*The Word Among Us*, Lent 2002

Reflect!

1. On the first Passover, God directed the Israelites to sprinkle the blood of an unblemished lamb on the lintel and doorposts of their houses: "The blood shall be a sign for you on the houses where

you live: when I see the blood, I will pass over you, and no plague shall destroy you when I strike the land of Egypt" (Exodus 12:13).

The Passover lamb of the Old Testament foreshadowed Christ, the "paschal" or Passover lamb sacrificed for us (1 Corinthians 5:7), a "lamb without defect or blemish" (1 Peter 1:19) that was slain for our sins (Revelation 5:6, 9; 13:8). Christians see their Passover fulfilled in Jesus' "passing over" death to new life in the resurrection, rescuing his people with him. We have been saved from sin and from the meaninglessness of death to new life by the blood of Christ, the perfect sacrificial lamb.

Pray the hymn of Revelation 5:12-14 in praise of Jesus as the Lamb of God. How does your recognition of Jesus as the sacrificial lamb deepen your relationship with him?

2. Read the following passages prayerfully to help you better grasp what was accomplished by Christ when he shed his blood:

> Since all have sinned and fall short of the glory of God; they are now justified by his grace as a gift, through the redemption that is in Christ Jesus, whom God put forward as a sacrifice of atonement by his blood, effective through faith. (Romans 3:23-25)

> We have redemption through his blood, the forgiveness of our trespasses, according to the riches of his grace that he lavished on us. (Ephesians 1:7-8)

> In [Christ] all the fullness of God was pleased to dwell, and through him God was pleased to reconcile to himself all things, whether on earth or in heaven, by making peace through the blood of his cross. (Colossians 1:19-20)

There is one God;
> there is also one mediator between God and humankind,
Christ Jesus, himself human,
> who gave himself a ransom for all. (1 Timothy 2:5-6)

Christ did not enter a sanctuary made by human hands, a mere copy of the true one, but he entered into heaven itself, now to appear in the presence of God on our behalf. Nor was it to offer himself again and again, as the high priest enters the Holy Place year after year with blood that is not his own; for then he would have had to suffer again and again since the foundation of the world. But as it is, he has appeared once for all at the end of the age to remove sin by the sacrifice of himself. And just as it is appointed for mortals to die once, and after that the judgment, so Christ, having been offered once to bear the sins of many, will appear a second time, not to deal with sin, but to save those who are eagerly waiting for him. (Hebrews 9:24-28)

▶ In the Spotlight
Blood of Christ, Be Our Salvation

Blood of Christ, only Son of the Father,
> *be our salvation.*
Blood of Christ, incarnate Word,
> *be our salvation.*
Blood of Christ, that spilled to the ground,
> *be our salvation.*
Blood of Christ, that flowed at the scourging,
> *be our salvation.*
Blood of Christ, dripping from the thorns,
> *be our salvation.*

Blood of Christ, shed on the cross,
be our salvation.
Blood of Christ, the price of our redemption,
be our salvation.
Blood of Christ, our only claim to pardon,
be our salvation.
Blood of Christ, our blessing cup,
be our salvation.
Blood of Christ, in which we are washed,
be our salvation.
Blood of Christ, torrent of mercy,
be our salvation.
Blood of Christ, that overcomes evil,
be our salvation.
—Litany of the Precious Blood of Jesus

Act!

Meditate prayerfully on 1 John 1:7, 9: "The blood of Jesus . . . cleanses us from all sin. . . . If we confess our sins, he who is faithful and just will forgive us our sins and cleanse us from all unrighteousness."

Ask the Holy Spirit to help you make an honest and sincere examination of conscience. Then express to God your sorrow for your sins in an Act of Contrition, confident of the cleansing and healing power of Jesus' blood. If possible, receive the Sacrament of Reconciliation this week.

▶ In the Spotlight
The Pope Speaks

It is [the blood of Christ] that is the most powerful source of hope; indeed it is the foundation of the absolute certitude that in God's plan life will be victorious.

—**Pope John Paul II,** *Evangelium vitae*

The Eucharist . . . has a cosmic property: the transformation of the bread and wine into Christ's Body and Blood is in fact the principle of the divinization of creation itself.

—**Pope Benedict XVI,** Angelus Address, June 18, 2006

[Christ] did not merely say: "This is my body," "this is my blood," but went on to add: "which is given for you," "which is poured out for you" (Luke 22:19-20). Jesus did not simply state that what he was giving them to eat and drink was his body and his blood; he also expressed *its sacrificial meaning* and made sacramentally present his sacrifice which would soon be offered on the Cross for the salvation of all. "The Mass is at the same time, and inseparably, the sacrificial memorial in which the sacrifice of the Cross is perpetuated and the sacred banquet of communion with the Lord's body and blood" [*Catechism of the Catholic Church*, 1382].

—**Pope John Paul II,** *Ecclesia de eucharistia*

The fact that "expiation" flows from the "blood" of Christ signifies that it is not man's sacrifices that free him from the weight of his faults, but the loving act of God who opens Himself in the extreme.

—**Pope Benedict XVI,** Message for Lent 2010

"I Live by Faith in the Son of God"

Romans 5:6-11

6 While we were still weak, at the right time Christ died for the ungodly. 7Indeed, rarely will anyone die for a righteous person—though perhaps for a good person someone might actually dare to die. 8But God proves his love for us in that while we still were sinners Christ died for us. 9Much more surely then, now that we have been justified by his blood, will we be saved through him from the wrath of God. 10For if while we were enemies, we were reconciled to God through the death of his Son, much more surely, having been reconciled, will we be saved by his life. 11But more than that, we even boast in God through our Lord Jesus Christ, through whom we have now received reconciliation.

> The scale of God's love for us can be seen in the "reconciliation" which took place on the Cross, . . . when Christ did away with this enmity, making our peace with God and reconciling us to him.
> —*The Navarre Bible*

Galatians 2:19-20; 6:14

2:19I have been crucified with Christ; 20and it is no longer I who live, but it is Christ who lives in me. And the life I now live in the flesh I live by faith in the Son of God, who loved me and gave himself for me.

6:14May I never boast of anything except the cross of our Lord Jesus Christ, by which the world has been crucified to me, and I to the world.

G od proves his love for us in that while we still were sinners Christ died for us" (Romans 5:8). How wondrous it is that God has loved us so profoundly! The truth is that nothing about us could have merited God's love—not our strengths, talents, or accomplishments. Nor can our sins and weaknesses deter God from showing us mercy and redeeming us. As St. Augustine once put it, "Christ loved us in our unloveliness, in order to make us beautiful like himself." It's God's unconditional, generous love for us—which is his motivation for saving us—that we find at the heart of the gospel.

When we were entrapped in sin, Jesus died for us in an act of pure love. God's dealings with his chosen people Israel were a foreshadowing of this:

> It was not because you were more numerous than any other people that the LORD set his heart on you and chose you—for you were the fewest of all peoples. It was because the LORD loved you and kept the oath that he swore to your ancestors, that the LORD has brought you out with a mighty hand, and redeemed you from the house of slavery, from the hand of Pharaoh king of Egypt. (Deuteronomy 7:7-8)

Through Jesus' death, the whole human race—weak and ungodly as we are—has been pardoned. Our relationship with the Father, broken by Adam's sin, has been restored. That is what Paul means when he says that we are "reconciled to God" (Romans 5:10). We had been "enemies" (5:10) of God, but now "in Christ God was reconciling the world to himself, not counting their trespasses against them" (2 Corinthians 5:19). Jesus, the righteous and sinless one, took our sins upon himself on the cross "so that in him we might become the righteousness of God" (5:21). None of us have anything to boast of in ourselves; rather, with

> When we were entrapped in sin, Jesus died for us in an act of pure love.

grateful hearts we are to "boast in God through our Lord Jesus Christ, through whom we have now received reconciliation" (Romans 5:11). Yet although we have been reconciled to God, we are still in the process of being "saved" by Christ's life (5:10). Now Christ dwells in us, and day by day, the Spirit touches our hearts and minds in order to transform our disordered emotions and sinful thoughts—thus bringing Christ's full salvation into every area of our lives and making us "beautiful like himself." As we cooperate with this work, we'll grow to look more and more like Jesus.

Paul described this process in a similar way in his letter to the Galatians: "I have been crucified with Christ; and it is no longer I who live, but it is Christ who lives in me. And the life I now live in the flesh I live by faith in the Son of God" (2:19-20). In other words, putting aside the "old nature," the selfish ego, we are to "put on the Lord Jesus Christ and make no provision for the flesh, to gratify its desires" (Romans 13:14; see also Ephesians 4:22-24). When we put our faith in Christ and the power released in us by his cross, we receive the grace to overcome our tendency to sin. We will be able to break free from sinful patterns, addictions, or even habitual anxiety or fear—anything that binds us and prevents us from living the abundant life that Christ won for us. And we will be able to put on virtue and holiness, much in the way that Jesus put on a glorified body in his resurrection.

Paul's boast and confidence is in the redemption brought about by the passion and death of Jesus. No matter how shocking or scandalous it might have been to Jewish Christians of his day, Paul assured them that neither circumcision nor external observance of the law but only faith in the cross of Christ can save us (Galatians 6:12-15). In words that echo Paul's and ring with the same conviction, St. John Chrysostom declared:

> And what is the boast of the Cross? That Christ for my sake took on Him the form of a slave, and bore His sufferings for me the slave, the enemy, the unfeeling one; yea He

so loved me as to give Himself up to a curse for me. What can be comparable to this! . . . Let us then not be ashamed of His unspeakable tenderness; He was not ashamed of being crucified for your sake, and will you be ashamed to confess His infinite solicitude? (*Homily 6 on Galatians*)

May we too, like Paul, base our lives on faith in Christ and boast not of ourselves but of the incomparable love of Christ for us and of the saving power of his cross!

Understand!

1. Why do you think Paul makes such a point of emphasizing that Christ died "while we were still weak," for the "ungodly" (Romans 5:6)? Why is this such a crucial issue for us to understand?

_____

_____

_____

_____

_____

2. What does it mean to be an enemy of God (Romans 5:10)? What does St. James say about being an enemy of God in his epistle (4:4)? How is a change in this status and reconciliation with God brought about?

_____

_____

_____

_____

_____

3. Why was it important to Paul that he be crucified to "the world" (Galatians 6:14)? Read John 15:19, Romans 12:2, and 1 John 2: 15-17. What sense do you get from these passages about what Paul means by "the world"? How does this differ from the world God created, which is "good" (Genesis 1:31)?

----

4. "The life I now live in the flesh I live by faith in the Son of God" (Galatians 2:20). From this verse and Paul's argument to the Jews in Galatians 6:12-15, describe the role and importance of faith and what it accomplishes in you.

----

5. What is the "good news" of these passages from St. Paul? How would you explain it concisely to someone who does not know Christ?

The Sign of the Cross, Holiest of All Signs

Tracing the sign of the cross on one's forehead with the thumb was a custom practiced in private devotion and in liturgical and sacramental functions as early as the second century. Making the sign of the cross on the forehead, breast, and shoulders with two fingers folded toward the palm (recalling the divine and human natures of Christ) and two fingers and thumb extended (recalling the Trinity) was introduced in the sixth century. The custom, with slight variations in form and use, eventually evolved in the Western Church to the form Roman Catholics use today: the whole hand with fingers extended and the shoulders touched from left to right.

The most ancient words to accompany the sign of the cross are the invocation "In the name of the Father, and of the Son, and of the Holy Spirit." In the Eastern rites, one of the invocations frequently used is "Holy God, holy strong One, holy immortal One, have mercy on us."

Making the sign of the cross is an outward sign of our faith, a physical declaration that we belong to Christ, and a radical act of devotion.

When we cross ourselves, let it be with a real sign of the cross. Instead of a small cramped gesture that gives no notion of its meaning, let us make a large unhurried sign, from forehead to breast, from shoulder to shoulder, consciously feeling how it includes the whole of us, our thoughts, our attitudes, our body and soul, every part of us at once, how it consecrates and sanctifies us.

It does so because it is the sign of the universe and the sign of our redemption. On the cross Christ redeemed mankind. By the cross he sanctifies man to the last shred and fiber of his being. We make the sign of the cross before we pray to collect and compose ourselves and to fix our minds and hearts and wills upon God. We make it when we finish praying in order that we may hold fast the gift we have received from God. In temptations we sign ourselves to be strengthened; in dangers, to be protected. The cross is signed upon us in blessings in order that the fullness of God's life may flow into the soul and fructify and sanctify us wholly.

Think of these things when you make the sign of the cross. It is the holiest of all signs. Make a large cross, taking time, thinking what you do. Let it take in your whole being,—body, soul, mind, will, thoughts, feelings, your doing and not-doing,—and by signing it with the cross strengthen and consecrate the whole in the strength of Christ, in the name of the triune God.

—**Roman Guardini,** *Sacred Signs*

Grow!

1. Recall an instance when you were particularly aware of God loving you in your "unloveliness"—with all your failings, sins, and weaknesses. How did this realization affect you? How did you respond to God?

_____

_____

_____

_____

_____

_____

2. In what ways are you "saved" by the cross (Romans 5:9, 10)? What were you saved from? What were you saved for? How do you live out this truth in your everyday life?

_____

_____

_____

_____

_____

_____

3. In what do you take personal pride or attempt to find your identity and security? Why? How might this change if you truly sought your identity and security only in God and what he has accomplished for you on the cross (Romans 5:11; Galatians 6:14)?

_____

_____

_____

_____

_____

_____

4. Do you find it difficult to identify with Paul's statement "I have been crucified with Christ; and it is no longer I who live, but it is Christ who lives in me" (Galatians 2:19-20)? Why or why not? In what ways have you put off your old nature and been "crucified to the world" (6:14)?

_____

_____

_____

_____

_____

_____

5. Think back to a time when you were reconciled with someone after an argument or a break in a relationship. How did it make you feel? How does an understanding of what God did for us in Christ help us to become more eager to seek forgiveness and reconciliation?

_____

_____

_____

_____

_____

_____

▶ **In the Spotlight**
"I Live Now, Not I, But Christ
Lives in Me"

At the age of fifteen, John Gabriel Perboyre believed that God was calling him to be a missionary to China. A year later he entered the seminary of the Congregation of the Mission, the Lazarists, in Montauban, France. He was ordained to the priesthood in 1825, and after serving as a seminary professor for nine years was sent to China in 1834.

During persecutions that arose a few years later against Christians, Fr. Perboyre was imprisoned. Twenty times Chinese authorities demanded that he trample on a crucifix and inform on his colleagues, and twenty times he refused, each time enduring brutal torture. He was even branded on his face with Chinese characters that proclaimed he was "a teacher of false religion." On September 11, 1840, John Gabriel was strangled to death. He was canonized in 1996 by Pope John Paul II.

The following prayer was written by St. John Gabriel Perboyre when he was twenty-three. He prayed it frequently throughout his life. It reflects his wish to be Christlike, a desire fulfilled in his life and death:

> O my Divine Savior, transform me into yourself. May my hands be the hands of Jesus. May my tongue be the tongue of Jesus. Grant that every faculty of my body may serve only to glorify you. Above all transform my soul and all its powers that my memory, my will, and my affections may be the memory, the will, and the affections of Jesus. I pray you to destroy in me all that is not of you. Grant that I may live but in you, and by you, and for you that I may truly say with St. Paul: "I live now, not I, but Christ lives in me" (Galatians 2:20).

Reflect!

1. When you make the sign of the cross, do you do so reverently and with a conscious affirmation of your faith? These words from St. John Chrysostom can help you make this prayer a true act of faith:

> When you sign yourself, think of all the mysteries contained in the cross. It is not enough to form it with the fingers. You must first make it with faith and good will. . . . When you mark your breast, your eyes, and all your members with the sign of the cross, offer yourself as a victim pleasing to God.

2. Reflect on the following passages to help you grasp more fully what it means that you have been reconciled with God through Christ:

> There is therefore now no condemnation for those who are in Christ Jesus. For the law of the Spirit of life in Christ Jesus has set you free from the law of sin and of death. For

God has done what the law, weakened by the flesh, could not do: by sending his own Son in the likeness of sinful flesh, and to deal with sin, he condemned sin in the flesh, so that the just requirement of the law might be fulfilled in us, who walk not according to the flesh but according to the Spirit. . . . If the Spirit of him who raised Jesus from the dead dwells in you, he who raised Christ from the dead will give life to your mortal bodies also through his Spirit that dwells in you. (Romans 8:1-4, 11)

God . . . reconciled us to himself through Christ, and has given us the ministry of reconciliation; that is, in Christ God was reconciling the world to himself, not counting their trespasses against them, and entrusting the message of reconciliation to us. So we are ambassadors for Christ, since God is making his appeal through us; we entreat you on behalf of Christ, be reconciled to God. For our sake he made him to be sin who knew no sin, so that in him we might become the righteousness of God. (2 Corinthians 5:18-21)

By grace you have been saved through faith, and this is not your own doing; it is the gift of God—not the result of works, so that no one may boast. (Ephesians 2:8-9)

Now in Christ Jesus you who once were far off have been brought near by the blood of Christ. For he is our peace; in his flesh he has made both groups [Gentiles and Jews] into one and has broken down the dividing wall, that is, the hostility between us. He has abolished the law with its commandments and ordinances, that he might create in himself one new humanity in place of the two, thus making peace, and might reconcile both groups to God in one body through the cross, thus putting to death that hostility through it. (Ephesians 2:13-16)

▶ In the Spotlight
The Precious and Life-Giving
Cross of Christ

How precious the gift of the cross, how splendid to contemplate! In the cross there is no mingling of good and evil, as in the tree of paradise: it is wholly beautiful to behold and good to taste. The fruit of this tree is not death but life, not darkness but light. This tree does not cast us out of paradise, but opens the way for our return.

This was the tree on which Christ, like a king on a chariot, destroyed the devil, the lord of death, and freed the human race from his tyranny. This was the tree upon which the Lord, like a brave warrior wounded in hands, feet and side, healed the wounds of sin that the evil serpent had inflicted on our nature. A tree once caused our death, but now a tree brings life. Once deceived by a tree, we have now repelled the cunning serpent by a tree. What an astonishing transformation! That death should become life, that decay should become immortality, that shame should become glory! Well might the holy Apostle exclaim: *Far be it from me to glory except in the cross of our Lord Jesus Christ, by which the world has been crucified to me, and I to the world!* The supreme wisdom that flowered on the cross has shown the folly of worldly wisdom's pride. The knowledge of all good, which is the fruit of the cross, has cut away the shoots of wickedness. . . .

By the cross death was slain and Adam was restored to life. The cross is the glory of all the apostles, the crown of the martyrs, the sanctification of the saints. By the cross we put on Christ and cast aside our former self. By the cross we, the sheep of Christ, have been gathered into one flock, destined for the sheepfold of heaven.

—**St. Theodore the Studite,** *Oratio in adorationem crucis*

Act!

Every Christian is called to share the saving news of the gospel with others. As Pope Paul VI wrote in his apostolic exhortation *Evangelii nuntiandi* [On Evangelization in the Modern World]:

> The Good News proclaimed by the witness of life sooner or later has to be proclaimed by the word of life. There is no true evangelization if the name, the teaching, the life, the promises, the kingdom, and the mystery of Jesus of Nazareth, the Son of God are not proclaimed. (22)

This week tell a family member, friend, neighbor, co-worker, or professional colleague what Christ has done in your life. Ask the Spirit to guide you in choosing whom to share with and to bless your words. Then speak naturally and sincerely—and with conviction and humility—about God's work in you. After your conversation, remember to keep this person in your prayers.

Taking time to review your personal testimony and to consider how to explain the gospel message simply can help you be more prepared and at ease when you speak to others about the Lord. As St. Peter advised, "Always be ready to give an explanation to anyone who asks you for a reason for your hope" (1 Peter 3:15, NAB).

▶ In the Spotlight
Glorying in the Cross of Christ

When she was officially declared a saint of the Church in 1998, Pope John Paul II described Edith Stein, a victim of the Holocaust, this way:

> St. Paul's words to the Galatians are well suited to the human and spiritual experience of Teresa Benedicta of the Cross. . . . She too can repeat with the Apostle: "Far be it from me to glory except in the Cross of our Lord Jesus Christ" (Galatians 6:14). . . . The mystery of the Cross gradually enveloped her whole life, spurring her to the point of making the supreme sacrifice.

Born into a German Jewish family in 1891, Edith studied philosophy and was known for her brilliance as a professor of phenomenology. She had abandoned Judaism as a teenager and was a self-proclaimed atheist. However, while staying with a Christian friend, Edith was impressed by the calm faith that sustained the woman at the death of her husband. Later she wrote:

> It was my first encounter with the Cross and the divine power that it bestows on those who carry it. For the first time, I was seeing with my very eyes the Church born from its Redeemer's sufferings, triumphant over the sting of death. That was the moment my unbelief collapsed and Christ shone forth—in the mystery of the Cross.

Edith was baptized in the Catholic Church in 1922. Ten years later she became a Carmelite nun. As Hitler rose to power, Edith was quick to perceive what this might cost her, her family, and her race, so she chose her religious name, Sr. Teresa Benedicta of the Cross, anticipating that she would share in the Lord's sufferings.

As the situation worsened for Jews in Germany, Sr. Teresa Benedicta knew she was not safe in the Cologne monastery and also believed that her presence there put all the nuns in danger. On the night of December 31, 1938, she crossed into the Netherlands, where she was received at the Carmel in Echt. Her sister Rosa, who had also become a Catholic, later followed her and served as a lay portress at the monastery. However, the Nazis occupied the Netherlands in 1940, and Jews, even those who were converts to Christianity, were no longer safe there either.

Sr. Teresa Benedicta and Rosa were arrested on August 2, 1942, as part of Hitler's orders to liquidate all non-Aryan Catholics in retaliation for a pastoral letter issued by the Dutch bishops that protested Nazi policies. As the two were taken from the convent, Sr. Teresa was heard to say to her sister, "Come, Rosa, let us go for our people." Their lives ended a week later in the gas chamber at Auschwitz, but her example lives on: She embraced the cross, and like Christ, it is where she found her glory.

"A New Creation"

Romans 6:3-14

[3]Do you not know that all of us who have been baptized into Christ Jesus were baptized into his death? [4]Therefore we have been buried with him by baptism into death, so that, just as Christ was raised from the dead by the glory of the Father, so we too might walk in newness of life.

[5] For if we have been united with him in a death like his, we will certainly be united with him in a resurrection like his. [6]We know that our old self was crucified with him so that the body of sin might be destroyed, and we might no longer be enslaved to sin. [7]For whoever has died is freed from sin. [8]But if we have died with Christ, we believe that we will also live with him. [9]We know that Christ, being raised from the dead, will never die again; death no longer has dominion over him. [10]The death he died, he died to sin, once for all; but the life he lives, he lives to God. [11]So you also must consider yourselves dead to sin and alive to God in Christ Jesus.

> They are happy who, putting all their trust in the cross, have plunged into the water of life.
> —Second-century author

[12] Therefore, do not let sin exercise dominion in your mortal bodies, to make you obey their passions. [13]No longer present your members to sin as instruments of wickedness, but present yourselves to God as those who have been brought from death to life, and present your members to God as instruments of righteousness. [14]For sin will have no dominion over you, since you are not under law but under grace.

2 Corinthians 5:17

[17]If anyone is in Christ, there is a new creation: everything old has passed away; see, everything has become new!

Galatians 5:1

¹ For freedom Christ has set us free. Stand firm, therefore, and do not submit again to a yoke of slavery.

Before Christ's incarnation, sin and death ruled over humanity's fallen nature, and no one could break their stranglehold on us. But Christ took on our human nature—becoming flesh and blood like us—"so that through death he might destroy the one who has the power of death, that is, the devil, and free those who all their lives were held in slavery by the fear of death" (Hebrews 2:14-15).

We were alienated from God, and death and sin infected humankind through the disobedience of Adam: "Sin came into the world through one man, and death came through sin, and so death spread to all because all have sinned" (Romans 5:12). But this infection was counteracted by the obedience and righteousness of Christ. For "just as one man's [Adam's] trespass led to condemnation for all, so one man's [Christ's] act of righteousness leads to justification and life for all" (5:18). His act and its significance are so profound that Jesus is frequently called the "new" or "last" Adam, the beginning of a new creation and a "life-giving spirit" (1 Corinthians 15:22, 45).

By his crucifixion and resurrection, Christ delivered us from the power of Satan, slavery to sin, and fear of death. When we are united with Christ's death and resurrection through baptism, we actually experience this freedom, for we enter into communion with Christ, are buried with him, and rise to newness of life with him (Romans 6:3-4). As St. Basil the Great explains, spiritually we

> imitate Christ's death by being buried with him in baptism. If we ask what this kind of burial means and what benefit we may hope to derive from it, it means first of all making a complete

break with our former way of life, and our Lord himself said that this cannot be done unless a man is born again. In other words, we have to begin a new life, and we cannot do so until our previous life has been brought to an end. When runners reach the turning point on a racecourse, they have to pause briefly before they can go back in the opposite direction. So also when we wish to reverse the direction of our lives there must be a pause, or a death, to mark the end of one life and the beginning of another. (*On the Holy Spirit*)

"Christ has set us free" (Galatians 5:1). Now we are "a new creation" (2 Corinthians 5:17). However, there is a difference between knowing these truths and seeing them applied in our lives. Concretely experiencing this freedom and newness of life depends upon our allowing the cross to do its work in us, breaking the strongholds of sin and replacing them with the fruits of the Holy Spirit. It is as we remind ourselves that "our old self was crucified with [Christ] so that the body of sin might be destroyed, and we might no longer be enslaved to sin" (Romans 6:6) that the power of the cross is released in us. It is as we place our faith and trust in Jesus' cross that our slavery to sin—our bondage to anger, jealousies, and lying, to immoral patterns and harmful addictions—is broken.

> Baptism is a crucifixion of our sinful condition, so that the "old self" no longer controls our behavior.

To live a life filled with the power of the cross and with baptismal grace—a life in which "sin will have no dominion over [us]" (Romans 6:14)—we must let go of our past way of life and open ourselves to God's grace and transforming power. Although our dying is spiritual and symbolic—we have not been physically nailed to the cross as Jesus was—it is not simply theoretical. In a real way, we must commit ourselves to enact and actualize the "death" of our baptism daily, allowing our sinful nature to be crucified with Christ. In other words, baptism is a crucifixion of our sinful condition, so that the "old self" no longer controls our behavior. And the fruit of baptism is "a rich reality that includes forgiveness of original sin and all personal sins, birth into the new life by which man becomes an adoptive son of the Father, a member of Christ and a temple of the Holy Spirit" (*Catechism of the Catholic Church*, 1279).

Paul's great declaration in Romans 6:3-11 is proclaimed each year at the Easter Vigil, following the seven Old Testament readings that recount our salvation history. The third reading in particular—Exodus 14:15–15:1, which describes Israel's deliverance from the oppression of the Egyptian Pharaoh through God's miraculous parting of the Red Sea—foreshadows our deliverance from sin and death and the transformation effected in us by baptism. It is also, fittingly, at the Easter Vigil that the waters of the baptismal font are blessed, catechumens are baptized—dying and rising with Christ—and received into the Church, and the faithful renew their baptismal vows, rejecting Satan and all his works and empty promises, as well as sin and the glamour of evil, and resolving to live with Christ.

Understand!

1. According to St. Paul, how are we "united with [Christ] in a death like his" (Romans 6:5)? What are the consequences of this union?

_____

_____

_____

_____

_____

_____

2. Note all the expressions that Paul uses to describe the effects and fruits of being buried with Christ in baptism. What dominant theme do you find in all these expressions?

_____

_____

_____

_____

_____

_____

3. Why does death no longer have dominion over humankind (see Romans 6:8-9)?

_____

_____

_____

_____

_____

4. "There is a new creation: everything old has passed away; see, everything has become new!" (2 Corinthians 5:17). Do you think that Paul's statement is an apt description of what is accomplished in us when we put our faith in the power of the cross? In what way do you think that Paul had personal experience of this truth?

_____

_____

_____

_____

_____

5. Explain in your own words what Paul means when he says that we are to "no longer present [our] members to sin as instruments of wickedness, but present [ourselves] to God as those who have been brought from death to life, and present [our] members to God as instruments of righteousness" (Romans 6:13). What happens when we follow Paul's exhortation?

_____

_____

_____

_____

_____

_____

▶ In the Spotlight
Baptized into Christ's Death

Being baptized into the death of Christ means having Christ dwell in us, now glorious and raised "through the glory of the Father." In his power we are able to die to sin. The word *sin* refers not primarily to our individual acts of sin but to the whole regime of sin, that complex of human rebellion and inhumanity that finds expression in the structures of the whole mode of life that characterizes "the world." When we die to sin, we are free of the power of that complex of social, political, cultural, economic, psychological, and spiritual forces that rule the world.

Our individual acts of sin are the ways in which we connive in and yield to these forces. We appropriate sin and make it our own. Paul tells us [in Romans 6:6-11] that we are free from this power if we consent to the new power at work in us. Jesus Christ, by his love and obedience in death, died to the forces that make up sin in the world. Because he lives in us, we, too, have been transferred to a new realm of existence. We can experience this, not as a theory, but as an actual fact, if we call upon that power when we are faced with those memories and habits of sin that keep us slaves to sin.

—**Francis Martin**, *The Fire in the Cloud: Lenten Meditations*

Grow!

1. Choose several adjectives that you feel characterize you as a "new creation" (2 Corinthians 5:17) in Christ. What word best explains what has been accomplished in your life through the Sacrament of Baptism?

_____

_____

_____

_____

_____

2. In what areas of your life do you most need or want to experience God's power setting you free? How might God help you (perhaps through prayer, confession, spiritual direction, a trusted friend, professional help, etc.) to break a sinful pattern or overcome a habitual failing?

_____

_____

_____

_____

_____

3. In what concrete ways have you already "died with Christ" to sin and broken with your old life? In what ways has Jesus set you free? How can you best nurture this new life in you?

_____

_____

_____

_____

_____

_____

4. How often do you turn to the cross to be set free from habits and attitudes that, although not sinful in themselves, keep you from experiencing new life in Christ? What are some things that particularly plague you (perhaps excessive anxiety, fear, pessimism, negativity)? When you are beset with such attitudes, how could turning to a crucifix help you?

_____

_____

_____

_____

_____

_____

5. Why is it significant that the Church celebrates a renewal of baptismal vows with the congregation each year during the Easter liturgy? How can this renewal help us to deepen our relationship with Christ?

_____

_____

_____

_____

_____

_____

▶ In the Spotlight
Save Us, O Holy Cross

Holy Cross where the Lamb of God was offered,
Save us, O Holy Cross.

Hope of Christians,
Save us, O Holy Cross.

Pledge of the resurrection of the dead,
Save us, O Holy Cross.

Shelter of persecuted innocence,
Save us, O Holy Cross.

Guide of the blind,
Save us, O Holy Cross.

Way of those who have gone astray,
Save us, O Holy Cross.

Staff of the lame,
Save us, O Holy Cross.

Consolation of the poor,
Save us, O Holy Cross.

Restraint of the powerful,
Save us, O Holy Cross.

Destruction of the proud,
Save us, O Holy Cross.

Refuge of sinners,
Save us, O Holy Cross.

Trophy of victory over Hell,
Save us, O Holy Cross.
—**Litany of the Holy Cross**

Reflect!

1. In his *Homily on Romans,* St. John Chrysostom notes: "So as to stay dead to sin after Baptism, personal effort is called for, although God's grace continues to be with us, providing us with great help."

   Reflect on the effects of the Sacrament of Baptism in your own life, and ask God for his grace and help in making the personal effort "to stay dead to sin" that John Chrysostom urges.

2. Read and meditate on the following passages to increase your awareness and appreciation of how God has set you free from slavery to sin through the sacrifice of Christ:

   > Therefore, just as sin came into the world through one man, and death came through sin, and so death spread to all because all have sinned—sin was indeed in the world before the law, but sin is not reckoned when there is no law. Yet death exercised dominion from Adam to Moses, even over those whose sins were not like the transgression of Adam, who is a type of the one who was to come.
   >   But the free gift is not like the trespass. For if the many died through the one man's trespass, much more surely have the grace of God and the free gift in the grace of the one man, Jesus Christ, abounded for the many. And the

free gift is not like the effect of the one man's sin. For the judgment following one trespass brought condemnation, but the free gift following many trespasses brings justification. If, because of the one man's trespass, death exercised dominion through that one, much more surely will those who receive the abundance of grace and the free gift of righteousness exercise dominion in life through the one man, Jesus Christ.

Therefore just as one man's trespass led to condemnation for all, so one man's act of righteousness leads to justification and life for all. For just as by the one man's disobedience the many were made sinners, so by the one man's obedience the many will be made righteous. But law came in, with the result that the trespass multiplied; but where sin increased, grace abounded all the more, so that, just as sin exercised dominion in death, so grace might also exercise dominion through justification leading to eternal life through Jesus Christ our Lord. (Romans 5:12-21)

The message about the cross is foolishness to those who are perishing, but to us who are being saved it is the power of God. (1 Corinthians 1:18)

When you were dead in trespasses and the uncircumcision of your flesh, God made you alive together with him, when he forgave us all our trespasses, erasing the record that stood against us with its legal demands. He set this aside, nailing it to the cross. (Colossians 2:13-14)

Since, therefore, the children share flesh and blood, he himself likewise shared the same things, so that through death he might destroy the one who has the power of death, that is, the devil, and free those who all their lives were held in slavery by the fear of death. (Hebrews 2:14-15)

▶ In the Spotlight
Witnessing to the Power of the Cross

In this imperfect world, we often find that theory and reality don't always see eye to eye. For instance, we can know in a theoretical way that our old life of sin was crucified with Christ and that through faith in the cross, we can be set free from the power of sin. But when it comes to the reality of our daily lives, we can find ourselves subject to the same kinds of sins over and over again. Here is the story of a man who made the connection between theory and reality—and experienced the power that flows from Jesus' cross.

For twenty-five years, Jim had been a chain smoker. For most of that time, he tried countless strategies to kick his habit. He tried self-discipline. He made bets with his friends. He wore a nicotine patch. He even went to a retreat to help him quit. Eventually, after years of failed attempts, Jim resigned himself to being in the grip of this ugly habit.

A couple of years ago, however, a routine X-ray revealed a spot on one of Jim's lungs, and he grew worried. He didn't want to go back to the old failed attempts, but he knew he had to do something. That's when his wife, Janet, told their parish priest about Jim's X-ray. The priest told Janet that Jim didn't have to feel hopeless. He told her about Jesus' cross and about the freedom that Jim could experience if he turned to the Lord. He even gave her a simple prayer that she and Jim could pray: "Lord Jesus, we believe that you died to set us free. We ask you, by the power of your cross, to free Jim from his addiction. Jesus, we trust in you and in your love for us."

Jim and Janet prayed this simple prayer every morning and night. Jim also prayed it every couple of hours at work—especially when the urge to smoke was strong. As he got closer to the Lord through this prayer, Jim felt his desire to smoke gradually diminishing—to the point where it has been fifteen months since his last cigarette.

Jim's story has a message for anyone who struggles with addiction, whether to cigarettes, alcohol, food, or even sex. Whatever the bondage, simple prayers like the one Jim prayed can be very powerful weapons to help break the grip of addiction. God doesn't want to see his children in bondage. He is waiting for us to turn to him, to trust in the power of his cross, and to ask for the grace to be set free.
—*The Word Among Us,* Lent 2007

Act!

Set aside an hour or two of time to rest in a quiet place where you will not be interrupted by others. Clear your mind of distractions, and in the silence and stillness recall as many of the ways that Jesus has freed you from sin and healed you as you can.

Make a mental or written list of the victories Christ has won for you and how he has transformed you. Then, in response, pray in your own words a "litany of thanksgiving."

▶ In the Spotlight
Baptism Is a Symbol of Christ's Passion

You were led down to the font of holy baptism just as Christ was taken down from the cross and placed in the tomb which is before your eyes. Each of you was asked, "Do you believe in the name of the Father, and of the Son, and of the Holy Spirit?" You made the profession of faith that brings salvation, you were plunged into the water, and three times you rose again. This symbolized the three days Christ spent in the tomb.

As our Savior spent three days and three nights in the depths of the earth, so your first rising from the water represented the first day and your first immersion represented the first night. At night a man cannot see, but in the day he walks in the light. So when you were immersed in the water, it was like night for you and you could not see, but when you rose it was like coming into broad daylight. In the same instant you died and were born again; the saving water was both your tomb and your mother. . . .

It was not we who actually died, were buried and rose again. We only did these things symbolically, but we have been saved in actual fact. It is Christ who was crucified, who was buried and who rose again, and all this has been attributed to us. We share in his sufferings symbolically and gain salvation in reality. What boundless love for men! Christ' undefiled hands were pierced by the nails; he suffered the pain. I experience no pain, no anguish, yet by the share that I have in his sufferings, he freely grants me salvation.

—*Jerusalem Catecheses*

"Take Up Your Cross and Follow Me"

Matthew 16:24-27

24 Then Jesus told his disciples, "If any want to become my followers, let them deny themselves and take up their cross and follow me. 25For those who want to save their life will lose it, and those who lose their life for my sake will find it. 26For what will it profit them if they gain the whole world but forfeit their life? Or what will they give in return for their life?

27 "For the Son of Man is to come with his angels in the glory of his Father, and then he will repay everyone for what has been done."
(See also Mark 8:34-38 and Luke 9:23-27)

The Cross symbolizes the life of an apostle of Christ. It brings a strength and a truth that delights both soul and body, though sometimes it is hard, and one can feel the weight.
—St. Josemaría Escrivá,
The Forge

Mark 15:20-21

20Then [the soldiers] led [Jesus] out to crucify him.

21 They compelled a passer-by, who was coming in from the country, to carry his cross; it was Simon of Cyrene, the father of Alexander and Rufus.
(See also Matthew 27:31-32 and Luke 23:26)

Galatians 6:2

2Bear one another's burdens, and in this way you will fulfill the law of Christ.

"I f any want to become my followers, let them deny themselves and take up their cross and follow me" (Matthew 16:24). Most likely Jesus' followers had seen criminals and insurgents against Roman rule hanging on crosses along the roads of Palestine and knew the horrors and shame of this excruciatingly painful form of execution used by the Romans. So Jesus' challenging call to his disciples to "take up their cross" must have both scandalized and stunned them. Perhaps they wondered whether, at such a cost, they wanted to follow him after all.

Jesus' declaration of the conditions of discipleship came after he had foretold his death and resurrection. Peter reacted strongly; he took Jesus aside "and began to rebuke him, saying, 'God forbid it, Lord!'" (Matthew 16:22). But Jesus rebuked Peter, calling him "a stumbling block," for Peter was "setting [his] mind not on divine things but on human things" (16:23). The conditions of discipleship also require us to set our minds on divine things. As the nineteenth-century Spanish archbishop and missionary St. Anthony Mary Claret explained:

> The Christian who desires to follow Jesus carrying his cross must bear in mind that the name "Christian" means "bearer or imitator of Christ" and that if he wishes to bear that noble title worthily, he must above all do as Christ charges us in the Gospel; we must oppose or deny ourselves, take up the cross, and follow him.

"Deny"—*aparneomai* in the Greek of the New Testament—is a judicial term meaning to "disavow or abjure connection with someone or something." Thus, to deny *oneself* is to renounce self-interest; to disregard the gratification of one's own needs and desires; to relinquish one's own will to do the will of God, imitating Jesus who gave himself over to his Father's plans for our salvation in total trust. The evangelist Luke adds a detail not found in Matthew's or Mark's account of Jesus' words: "If any want to become my followers, let them deny themselves and take up their cross *daily* and follow me" (Luke 9:23, emphasis added). Following Jesus is a matter for everyday life—a life of perseverance and steadfastness. Faithful discipleship involves making decisions every day to live Jesus' way, not our own. This involves making numerous choices and resolutions, even small ones, to serve our brothers or sisters in need, even if that involves foregoing our own needs and preferences. To "take up the cross," we often have to die to self in these seemingly mundane, everyday ways.

In Jesus' time, the Romans required those who were to be crucified to carry the wooden crossbeam—usually behind the nape of the neck like a yoke—to the place of execution, where an upright beam (called in Latin *crux simplex* or *palus*) was already implanted in the ground. Or they shouldered a T-shaped cross formed of both a vertical and a horizontal beam. Roman soldiers had the right to press people into temporary public service, so they "compelled" Simon of Cyrene (modern Libya) to relieve Jesus of his burden, probably because he was so weakened by exhaustion and the loss of blood from the scourging (Matthew 27:31-32; Mark 15:20-21; Luke 23:26). It is noteworthy that we find the same term—in Greek, *angareuo*—in Jesus' Sermon on the Mount: "if anyone forces [*compels*, KJV] you to go one mile, go also the second mile" (Matthew 5:41). It is when we "bear one another's burdens" that we "fulfill the law of Christ" (Galatians 6:2).

> Faithful discipleship involves making decisions every day to live Jesus' way, not our own.

Thus conscripted, Simon of Cyrene literally took up the cross for Jesus' sake—and so through the past two millennia he has been looked to by Christians as a model of discipleship. His unexpected encounter with Jesus must have had a great impact on him, since the evangelist Mark's mention of Simon's sons Alexander and Rufus (15:21) would imply that they were known to the early Christian

Church. Through his service to Jesus, did Simon become a believer and a true and lasting disciple of his?

Called to be disciples of Christ, we are to follow in our master's path. Our threefold course of action—denying self, taking up the cross, and following Jesus—sets us decisively on the road to eternal life. For Jesus promised that "those who lose their life for [his] sake will find it" (Matthew 16:25). If we hold fast, an everlasting reward will be ours, for when he comes "with his angels in the glory of his Father, . . . he will repay everyone for what has been done" (16:27).

Understand!

1. Why, in your opinion, does Jesus require such radical steps of those who would follow him? Why does he state these requirements after his prediction of his passion? Why does Jesus connect the fate of the disciples with his own fate?

_____

_____

_____

_____

_____

_____

2. What images and thoughts would the expression "take up the cross" have brought to Jesus' followers' minds? Why do you think Jesus used this graphic expression?

_____

_____

_____

_____

3. Explain in your own words the paradox Jesus speaks of in Matthew 16:25—"those who want to save their life will lose it, and those who lose their life for my sake will find it." How does this truth affect your daily choices and your present life? Your perspective on the life to come?

---

4. "What will it profit them if they gain the whole world but forfeit their life? Or what will they give in return for their life?" (Matthew 16:26). Do you think Jesus makes his point effectively with this principle of profit and loss? Why or why not? What answers would you give Jesus if he asked you these same questions?

---

5. "The Son of Man is to come with his angels in the glory of his Father, and then he will repay everyone for what has been done" (Matthew 16:27). What does this verse indicate about the final judgment? On what basis will we be rewarded or held accountable? See Matthew 7:21-27 for additional insight into the conduct Jesus holds to be important.

_____

_____

_____

_____

_____

_____

▶ In the Spotlight
The Fifth Station:
Simon of Cyrene Takes Up Jesus' Cross

What irony—Christ's own had fled,
no friend to share the pain and lend him aid when he faltered.

Simon, a stranger:
Carefree and casual, you happened along the way that morning
and unexpectedly your life was changed forever.
The choice was not your own, yet not one to turn away from:
"It is not you who have chosen me, but I who have chosen
   you" (John 15:16).

What welled up within your heart
as the soldiers compelled you to shoulder this man's load?
Burning anger, resentment, bitterness to be so put upon
   and shamed?
Fear to be involved and identified

with one rejected and despised by others?
Or were you moved to pity,
glad then to bend your strong back to help?

It came to you unsought—yet what a privilege
to have eased his burden for even a short stretch of his way!

Dare I take up the cross with you, Simon, and follow?
What answer would you give me now?

"If any one forces you to go one mile, go with him two miles"
(Matthew 5:41, RSV).

"Bear one another's burdens, and so fulfill the law of Christ"
(Galatians 6:2, RSV).
—**Jeanne Kun,** *He Went This Way Before Us: The Stations of the Cross of Our Lord Jesus Christ*

Grow!

1. Recall an instance when you acted to "save" your life—when you did something that did not take God or his plan for your life into account—but then "lost" something important in the process. What did you learn from this experience?

_____

_____

_____

_____

_____

2. Consider some examples of how you do, in fact, deny yourself, "losing" your life to "find" it. How do you see the truth of this paradox at work in your life? In your experience, what "gain" outweighs the costs of discipleship? What do you hope to gain in the future?

_____

_____

_____

_____

_____

_____

3. What is most challenging to you right now about the conditions of Jesus' call to be his disciple? What might you do to relieve your fears or reservations about denying yourself, taking up your cross, and following him?

_____

_____

_____

_____

_____

_____

4. In what ways do you identify with Simon of Cyrene? What does Simon's example teach you about discipleship? Have you ever been "compelled" to bear another person's "cross"? If so, what impact did this have on you?

_____

_____

_____

_____

_____

_____

5. Imagine how Jesus felt toward Simon. Has anyone ever helped you carry a burden you were struggling with? If so, how did you feel toward that person? What did you learn from this person's generosity and service to you?

_____

_____

_____

_____

_____

_____

▶ In the Spotlight
No Greater Love Than This

On the evening before his death, Jesus told his apostles, "No one has greater love than this, to lay down one's life for one's friends" (John 15:13). On the cross he gave them the example of ultimate love, dying for their sake and that of all humankind. From the earliest days of the Church to the present, countless followers of Jesus have taken his words and his example to heart, denying themselves and selflessly giving their lives for others.

In Auschwitz, the notoriously inhuman Nazi extermination camp, Franciscan priest Fr. Maximilian Kolbe volunteered to take the place of Francis Gajowniczek, a Polish soldier who had been chosen to be a victim of retaliatory execution for the escape of a prisoner. Fr. Kolbe told the Nazi commandant, "I am a Catholic priest from Poland; I would like to take his place because he has a wife and children." The commandant returned Gajowniczek to the camp ranks and confined Kolbe and nine other chosen prisoners in a starvation bunker. After being deprived of food and water for fourteen days, Kolbe and three others who were still alive were given lethal injections by the camp executioner on August 14, 1941. Pope John Paul II called Maximilian Kolbe a "martyr of love" and declared him a saint in 1982.

Another profound act of sacrificial love took place on April 30, 1997, when the African nation of Burundi was torn by ethnic wars. Hutu rebels invaded the small Catholic seminary in Buta. Armed with knives, machetes, clubs, and machine guns, the rebels told the young seminarians to divide into two ethnic groups, Hutus and Tutsis. Even though the Hutu students could have saved their lives by separating themselves from the Tutsis, they refused to abandon their classmates. Ultimately, the assailants massacred the forty-one Hutu and Tutsi companions together, "martyrs of brotherhood."

"No one has greater love than this, to lay down one's life for one's friends" (John 15:13).

Reflect!

1. Simon of Cyrene did not volunteer to carry Christ's cross, so this incident reminds us that sometimes "crosses" seem to be arbitrarily laid on us by life, burdens we might not of our own volition have chosen to carry. In Christian spirituality there is a sense in which "bearing our crosses" means accepting that through these crosses, God fosters our Christian growth and transforms us into his likeness. He is not the author of our difficulties and misfortunes or the cause of our pains, but he turns such things to his purposes for us and works through them. Meditate on the following words of saints who have recognized this, and let their perspective shape your outlook on your own personal crosses:

Let us bear our cross and leave it to God to determine the length and the weight.
—St. Rose Philippine Duchesne

You must accept your cross; if you carry it courageously
it will carry you to heaven.
—St. John Mary Vianney

2. Reflect on the following passages that challenge us to greater
   discipleship and selfless giving of ourselves to others in love and
   service:

> Now large crowds were traveling with [Jesus]; and he
> turned and said to them, "Whoever comes to me and does
> not hate father and mother, wife and children, brothers
> and sisters, yes, and even life itself, cannot be my disciple.
> Whoever does not carry the cross and follow me cannot
> be my disciple. For which of you, intending to build a
> tower, does not first sit down and estimate the cost, to see
> whether he has enough to complete it? Otherwise, when
> he has laid a foundation and is not able to finish, all who
> see it will begin to ridicule him, saying, 'This fellow began
> to build and was not able to finish.' Or what king, going
> out to wage war against another king, will not sit down
> first and consider whether he is able with ten thousand to
> oppose the one who comes against him with twenty thou-
> sand? If he cannot, then, while the other is still far away,
> he sends a delegation and asks for the terms of peace. So
> therefore, none of you can become my disciple if you do
> not give up all your possessions." (Luke 14:25-33)

> [Jesus said:] "Very truly, I tell you, unless a grain of wheat
> falls into the earth and dies, it remains just a single grain;
> but if it dies, it bears much fruit. Those who love their life
> lose it, and those who hate their life in this world will keep
> it for eternal life. Whoever serves me must follow me, and
> where I am, there will my servant be also. Whoever serves
> me, the Father will honor." (John 12:24-26)

You do well if you really fulfill the royal law according to the scripture, "You shall love your neighbor as yourself." (James 2:8)

Christ also suffered for you, leaving you an example, so that you should follow in his steps. (1 Peter 2:21)

▶ In the Spotlight
The Pope Speaks

When the Gospels use the verb "to follow," it means that where [Christ] goes, his disciple must also go. Thus, Christian life is defined as a life with Jesus Christ, a life to spend together with him.
—**Pope Benedict XVI,** General Audience, September 27, 2006

The Cross . . . is the extreme "yes" of God to man, the supreme expression of his love and the source of full and perfect life. It therefore contains the most convincing invitation to follow Christ on the way of gift of self.
—**Pope Benedict XVI,** Address to the Fourth National Ecclesial Convention, October 19, 2006

The purest joy lies in the relationship with [Christ], encountered, followed, known and loved, thanks to constant effort of mind and heart. To be a disciple of Christ: for a Christian this suffices.
—**Pope Benedict XVI,** Angelus Address, January 15, 2006

Whoever wants to be a friend of Jesus and become his authentic disciple—be it seminarian, priest, religious or lay person—must cultivate an intimate friendship with him in meditation and prayer.

—**Pope Benedict XVI,** Address to the Pontifical Roman Universities, October 23, 2006

Act!

"Bear one another's burdens, and in this way you will fulfill the law of Christ" (Galatians 6:2).

Reach out this week to someone in your parish, neighborhood, or workplace who is in need or weighed down in some way (for example, by illness, unemployment, loneliness, or difficult family relationships). Like Simon of Cyrene who relieved Jesus of his burden, help this person carry his or her cross. You might offer a word of encouragement, perform an act of kindness, do some practical service such as preparing a meal, or simply be present to share his or her sorrow. Be generous, not grudging, as you support and assist this person on his or her personal "way of the cross."

▶ In the Spotlight
The Royal Road of the Holy Cross

Why do you fear to take up the cross when through it you can win a kingdom? In the cross is salvation, in the cross is life, in the cross is protection from enemies, in the cross is infusion of heavenly sweetness, in the cross is strength of mind, in the cross is joy of spirit, in the cross is highest virtue, in the cross is perfect holiness. There is no salvation of soul nor hope of everlasting life but in the cross.

Take up your cross, therefore, and follow Jesus, and you shall enter eternal life. He himself opened the way before you in carrying his cross, and upon it, he died for you, that you, too, might take up your cross and long to die upon it. If you die with him, you shall also live with him, and if you share his suffering, you shall also share his glory.

—**Thomas à Kempis,** *The Imitation of Christ*

Practical Pointers for Bible Discussion Groups

A Bible discussion group is another key that can help us unlock God's word. Participating in a discussion or study group—whether through a parish, a prayer group, or a neighborhood—offers us the opportunity to grow not only in our love for God's word but also in our love for one another. We don't have to be trained Scripture scholars to benefit from discussing and studying the Bible together. Bible-study groups provide environments in which we can worship and pray together and strengthen our relationships with other Christians. The following guidelines can help a group get started and run smoothly.

Getting Started

- Decide on a regular time and place to meet. Meeting on a regular basis allows the group to maintain continuity without losing momentum from the previous discussion.

- Set a time limit for each session. An hour and a half is a reasonable length of time in which to have a rewarding discussion on the material contained in each of the sessions in this guide. However, the group may find that a longer time is even more advantageous. If it is necessary to limit the meeting to an hour, select sections of the material that are of greatest interest to the group.

- Designate a moderator or facilitator to lead the discussions and keep the meetings on schedule. This person's role is to help preserve good group dynamics by keeping the discussion on track. He or she should help ensure that no one monopolizes the session and that each person—including the shyest or quietest individual—is offered an opportunity to speak. The group may want to ask members to take turns moderating the sessions.

- Provide enough copies of the study guide for each member of the group, and ask everyone to bring a Bible to the meetings. Each session's Scripture text and related passages for reflection are printed in full in the guides, but you will find that a Bible is helpful for looking up other passages and cross-references. The translation provided in this guide is the New Revised Standard Version (Catholic Edition). You may also want to refer to other translations—for example, the New American Bible or the New Jerusalem Bible—to gain additional insights into the text.

- Try to stay faithful to your commitment and attend as many sessions as possible. Not only does regular participation provide coherence and consistency to the group discussions, it also demonstrates that members value one another and are committed to sharing their lives with one another.

Session Dynamics

- Read the material for each session in advance and take time to consider the questions and your answers to them. The single most important key to any successful Bible study is having everyone prepared to participate.

- As a courtesy to all members of your group, try to begin and end each session on schedule. Being prompt respects the other commitments of the members and allows enough time for discussion. If the group still has more to discuss at the end of the allotted time, consider continuing the discussion at the next meeting.

- Open the sessions with prayer. A different person could have the responsibility of leading the opening prayer at each session. The prayer could be a spontaneous one, a traditional prayer such as the Our Father, or one that relates to the topic of that particular meeting. The members of the group might also want to begin some of the meetings with a song or hymn. Whatever you choose, ask the Holy Spirit to guide your discussion and study of the Scripture text presented in that session.

- Contribute actively to the discussion. Let the members of the group get to know you, but try to stick to the topic so that you won't divert the discussion from its purpose. And resist the temptation to monopolize the conversation so that everyone will have an opportunity to learn from one another.

- Listen attentively to everyone in the group. Show respect for the other members and their contributions. Encourage, support, and affirm them as they share. Remember that many questions have more than one answer and that the experience of everyone in the group can be enriched by considering a variety of viewpoints.

- If you disagree with someone's observation or answer to a question, do so gently and respectfully, in a way that shows that you value the person who made the comment, and then explain your own point of view. For example, rather than say "You're wrong!" or "That's ridiculous!" try something like "I think I see what you're getting at, but I think that Jesus was saying something different in this passage." Be careful to avoid sounding aggressive or argumentative. Then, watch to see how the subsequent discussion unfolds. Who knows? You may come away with a new and deeper perspective.

- Don't be afraid of pauses and reflective moments of silence during the session. People may need some time to think about a question before putting their thoughts into words.

- Maintain and respect confidentiality within the group. Safeguard the privacy and dignity of each member by not repeating what has been shared during the discussion session unless you have been given permission to do so. That way everyone will get the greatest benefit out of the group by feeling comfortable enough to share on a deep, personal level.

- End the session with prayer. Thank God for what you have learned through the discussion, and ask him to help you integrate it into your life.

The Lord blesses all our efforts to come closer to him. As you spend time preparing for and meeting with your small group, be confident in the knowledge that Christ will fill you with wisdom, insight, and grace, and the ability to see him at work in your daily life.

Sources and Acknowledgments

Introduction

Nicene Creed, *The Catholic Source Book*, ed. Peter Klein (Dubuque, IA: Brown-Roa, 2000), 4.

Basil the Great, "On the Holy Spirit," quoted in *The Liturgy of the Hours, Volume II* (New York: Catholic Book Publishing Co., 1976), 441. Used with permission.

Richard John Neuhaus, *Death on a Friday Afternoon: Meditations on the Last Words of Jesus from the Cross* (New York: Basic Books, 2000), 29.

Thomas Aquinas, *About the Creed*, 6, quoted in Francis Fernandez, *In Conversation with God, Volume 2* (London: Scepter Ltd., 1989), 230.

Exsultet, http://www.catholic.org/prayers/prayer.php?p=641&cb300=vocations.

Session 1: Jesus' Crucifixion

John Paul II, *Letter to Priests*, Holy Thursday 1999, http://www.usccb.org/pope/thursday1999.htm.

Jean-Pierre Prévost, *God's Word Today*, (Volume 28, Number 6, June 2006), 30.

Frank Sheed, *To Know Christ Jesus* (San Francisco: Ignatius Press, 1992), 364.

Fulton J. Sheen, *The Life of Christ* (New York: Image Books/Doubleday, 1990), 383–384. Copyright © 1958, 1977 by Fulton J. Sheen. Used with permission of Doubleday, a division of Random House, Inc.

The Navarre Bible: The Pentateuch, with a commentary by the members of the Faculty of Theology of the University of Navarre (Dublin, Ireland: Four Courts Press, 1999), 118.

Bernard of Clairvaux, quoted in Jill Haak Adels, *The Wisdom of the Saints: An Anthology* (New York: Oxford University Press, 1987), 15.

Alphonsus Liguori, *The Passion and the Death of Jesus Christ*, quoted in *Divine Love Came Down! Wisdom from Saint Alphonsus Liguori*, ed. Nancy Sabbag (Ijamsville, MD: The Word Among Us Press, 2003), 51.

Teresa of Calcutta, quoted in *Love: A Fruit Always in Season* (San Francisco: Ignatius Press, 1987), 102.

Thérèse of Lisieux, *General Correspondence, Volume I* (Washington, DC: Institute of Carmelite Studies, 1982), 553.

Paul of the Cross, quoted in Paul Thigpen, *A Dictionary of Quotes from the Saints* (Ann Arbor, MI: Servant Publications, 2001), 32.

Session 2: The Triumph of the Cross

Easter Sequence, *Victimae Paschali Laudes,* quoted in Maria Boulding, *Prayer: Our Journey Home* (Ann Arbor, MI: Servant Books, 1980), 19.

Benedcit XVI, Homily, April 15, 2007, http://www.vatican.va/holy_father/ benedict_xvi/homilies/2007/documents/hf_ben-xvi_hom_20070415_80 -genetliaco_en.html.

Andrew of Crete, quoted in *Journey with the Saints* Desk Calendar (Ijamsville, MD: The Word Among Us Press, 2003), March 6.

Leo the Great, quoted in *Journey with the Saints*, March 9.

Ephrem of Syria, quoted in *Journey with the Saints*, March 10.

Damasus Winzen, *Pathways in Scripture* (Ann Arbor, MI: Servant Books, 1976), 76.

Benedict XVI, Letter to Cardinal Cordero Lanza di Montesemolo, November 25, 2006, http://www.vatican.va/holy_father/benedict_xvi/letters/2006/documents/ hf_ben-xvi_let_20061125_san-paolo_en.html.

Rupert of Deutz, *The Throne of Love,* http://www.rc.net/wcc/throne1.htm.

Session 3: Redeemed by Christ's Blood

Clement I, quoted in *The Book of Catholic Quotations,* ed. John Chapin (New York: Farrar, Straus and Cudahy, 1956), 104.

John Chrysostom, quoted in Paul Thigpen, *A Dictionary of Quotes from the Saints* (Ann Arbor, MI: Servant Publications, 2001), 31.

Council of Trent, 1562: DS 1743, quoted in the *Catechism of the Catholic Church* (San Francisco: Ignatius Press, 1994), no. 1367.

Ambrose, Commentary on Psalm 1, quoted in *Christian Spirituality: Origins to the Twelfth Century, Volume 1,* ed. Bernard McGinn, John Meyendorff, Jean Leclercq (New York: Crossroad Publishing Company, 1985), 370.

Augustine, Sermon 329, quoted in *The Liturgy of the Hours, Volume IV* (New York: Catholic Book Publishing Co., 1975), 1421. Used with permission.

Catherine of Siena, Letter 16, http://suburbanbanshee.wordpress.com/2009/09/17/ translation-from-letter-16-to-a-great-prelate-by-st-catherine-of-siena/.

Albert the Great, http://www.olmlaycarmelites.org/enews/2007/2007_issue3.html.

Benedict XVI, Homily at Vespers, July 4, 2009, http://www.vatican.va/holy_father/benedict_xvi/homilies/2009/documents/hf_ben-xvi_hom_20090704_cappella-paolina_en.html.

The Word Among Us, Lent 2002, 15–16.

Litany of the Precious Blood of Jesus, quoted in Peter Klein, *The Catholic Source Book* (Dubuque, IA: Brown-Roa, 2000), 22.

John Paul II, *Evangelium vitae* [The Gospel of Life], no. 25, http://www.vatican.va/edocs/ENG0141/_INDEX.HTM.

Benedict XVI, Angelus Address, June 18, 2006, http://www.vatican.va/holy_father/benedict_xvi/angelus/2006/documents/hf_ben-xvi_ang_20060618_en.html.

John Paul II, *Ecclesia de eucharistia* [On the Eucharist and Its Relationship to the Church], no. 12, http://www.vatican.va/holy_father/special_features/encyclicals/documents/hf_jp-ii_enc_20030417_ecclesia_eucharistia_en.html.

Benedict XVI, Message for Lent 2010, http://www.vatican.va/holy_father/benedict_xvi/messages/lent/documents/hf_ben-xvi_mes_20091030_lent-2010_en.html.

Session 4: Boasting in the Cross

The Navarre Bible: Romans and Galatians, with a commentary by the members of the Faculty of Theology of the University of Navarre (Dublin, Ireland: Four Courts Press, 1998), 97–98.

Augustine, Sermon on John 10:13, http://www.goodnews.ie/wisdomlinemar2006.shtml.

John Chrysostom, *Homily 6 on Galatians,* 14, http://www.newadvent.org/fathers/23106.htm.

Roman Guardini, *Sacred Signs,* "The Sign of the Cross," trans. Grace Branham (St. Louis, MO: Pio Decimo Press, 1956), http://www.ewtn.com/library/LITURGY/SACRSIGN.TXT.

John Gabriel Perboyre, quoted in Bert Ghezzi, *Voices of the Saints* (New York: Doubleday, 2000), 372.

John Chrysostom, quoted in Jean Joseph Gaume, *The Sign of the Cross in the Nineteenth Century,* trans. Daughter of St. Joseph (Philadelphia: Peter F. Cunningham, 1873), 323.

Theodore the Studite, *Oratio in adorationem crucis*, quoted in *The Liturgy of the Hours, Volume II* (New York: Catholic Book Publishing Co., 1976), 677–678. Used withs permission.

Paul VI, *Evangelii nuntiandi* [On Evangelization in the Modern World], no. 22, http://www.vatican.va/holy_father/paul_vi/apost_exhortations/documents/hf_p-vi _exh_19751208_evangelii-nuntiandi_en.html.

John Paul II, Homily at the Canonization of Edith Stein, October 11, 1998, http:// www.vatican.va/holy_father/john_paul_ii/homilies/1998/documents/hf_jp-ii _hom_11101998_stein_en.html.

Edith Stein, quoted in Waltraud Herbstrith, *Edith Stein: A Biography* (San Francisco: Ignatius, 1985), 56.

Session 5: Freedom from Sin and Death

Second-century author, quoted in *The Liturgy of the Hours, Volume III* (New York: Catholic Book Publishing Co., 1975), 684. Used by permission.

Basil the Great, "On the Holy Spirit," quoted in *The Liturgy of the Hours, Volume II* (New York: Catholic Book Publishing Co., 1976), 441. Used with permission.

Francis Martin, *The Fire in the Cloud: Lenten Meditations* (Ann Arbor, MI: Servant Publications, 2001), 144–145.

Litany of the Holy Cross, http://www.catholicdoors.com/prayers/litanies/p03498 .htm.

John Chrysostom, *Homily on Romans*, 11, quoted in *The Navarre Bible: Romans and Galatians*, with a commentary by the members of the Faculty of Theology of the University of Navarre (Dublin, Ireland: Four Courts Press, 1999), 104.

The Word Among Us, Lent 2007, 13–14.

Jerusalem Catecheses, quoted in *The Liturgy of the Hours, Volume II* (New York: Catholic Book Publishing Co., 1976), 596–597.

Session 6: Discipleship

Josemaría Escrivá, *The Forge*, quoted in Rosemary Ellen Guiley, *The Quotable Saint* (New York, NY: Checkmark Books, 2002), 45.

Anthony Mary Claret, quoted in Jill Haak Adels, *The Wisdom of the Saints: An Anthology* (New York: Oxford University Press, 1987), 73.

Jeanne Kun, *He Went This Way Before Us: The Stations of the Cross of Our Lord Jesus Christ* (unpublished manuscript).

Rose Philippine Duchesne, quoted in *Wisdom from Women Saints* Stand-up Calendar (Ijamsville, MD: The Word Among Us Press, 2008), March 18.

John Mary Vianney, quoted in *The Wisdom of the Saints: An Anthology*, 73.

Benedict XVI, General Audience, September 27, 2006, http://www.vatican.va/holy_father/benedict_xvi/audiences/2006/documents/hf_ben-xvi_aud_20060927_en.html.

Benedict XVI, Address to the Fourth National Ecclesial Convention, October 19, 2006, http://www.vatican.va/holy_father/benedict_xvi/speeches/2006/october/documents/hf_ben-xvi_spe_20061019_convegno-verona_en.html.

Benedict XVI, Angelus Address, January 15, 2006, http://www.vatican.va/holy_father/benedict_xvi/angelus/2006/documents/hf_ben-xvi_ang_20060115_en.html.

Benedict XVI, Address to the Pontifical Roman Universities, October 23, 2006, http://www.vatican.va/holy_father/benedict_xvi/speeches/2006/october/documents/hf_ben-xvi_spe_20061023_anno-accademico_en.html.

Thomas à Kempis, *The Imitation of Christ*, p. 9, trans. Aloysius Croft and Harold Bolton, http://www.bergen.edu/phr/121/KempisGC.pdf.

Also in The Word Among Us
Keys to the Bible Series

Six Sessions for Individuals or Groups

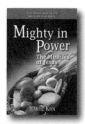

The Women of the Gospels: Missionaries of God's Love
Item# BTWFE9

Jesus' Journey to the Cross: A Love unto Death
Item# BTWGE9

Treasures Uncovered: The Parables of Jesus
Item# BTWAE5

Mighty in Power: The Miracles of Jesus
Item# BTWBE6

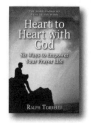

Food from Heaven: The Eucharist in Scripture
Item# BTWCE7

Heart to Heart with God: Six Ways to Empower Your Prayer Life
Item# BTWEE8

Moved by the Spirit: God's Power at Work in His People
Item# BTWDE8

Each of the Keys to the Bible study sessions features

- the full Scripture text;
- a short commentary;
- questions for reflection, discussion, and personal application;
- "In the Spotlight" sections featuring wisdom from the saints and the Church, root meanings of Greek words, fascinating historical background, and stories of faith from contemporary people.